Responsive Typography

Jason Pamental

Beijing · Cambridge · Farnham · Köln · Sebastopol · Tokyo

Responsive Typography

by Jason Pamental

Copyright © 2014 Jason Pamental. All rights reserved.

Printed in the United States of America.

Published by O'Reilly Media, Inc., 1005 Gravenstein Highway North, Sebastopol, CA 95472.

O'Reilly books may be purchased for educational, business, or sales promotional use. Online editions are also available for most titles (*http://my.safaribooksonline.com*). For more information, contact our corporate/institutional sales department: 800-998-9938 or *corporate@oreilly.com*.

Editors: Simon St. Laurent and Meghan Blanchette	**Indexer:** Last Look Editorial
Production Editor: Melanie Yarbrough	**Cover Designer:** Ellie Volckhausen
Copyeditor: Becca Freed	**Interior Designer:** David Futato
Proofreader: Eliahu Sussman	**Illustrator:** Rebecca Demarest

September 2014:   First Edition

Revision History for the First Edition:

2014-09-09:   First release

See *http://oreilly.com/catalog/errata.csp?isbn=9781491907092* for release details.

The O'Reilly logo is a registered trademark of O'Reilly Media, Inc. *Responsive Typography*, the cover image, and related trade dress are trademarks of O'Reilly Media, Inc.

Many of the designations used by manufacturers and sellers to distinguish their products are claimed as trademarks. Where those designations appear in this book, and O'Reilly Media, Inc. was aware of a trademark claim, the designations have been printed in caps or initial caps.

While the publisher and the author have used good faith efforts to ensure that the information and instructions contained in this work are accurate, the publisher and the author disclaim all responsibility for errors or omissions, including without limitation responsibility for damages resulting from the use of or reliance on this work. Use of the information and instructions contained in this work is at your own risk. If any code samples or other technology this work contains or describes is subject to open source licenses or the intellectual property rights of others, it is your responsibility to ensure that your use thereof complies with such licenses and/or rights.

ISBN: 978-1-491-90709-2

[LSI]

Dedicated to my darling wife Ellen, without whom I would be rudderless; to Trevor and Phoebe for always keeping me humble; and to Tristan, my constant companion on our wooded walks at sunrise.

Table of Contents

Part II. Getting Started with Web Fonts

Foreword

Back in my day, all we had was the `font` element.

I fully realize that makes me sound like an old man, but I'm not ready to chase young whippersnappers off my lawn quite yet. But the fact remains that when I taught myself how to build web pages back in the mid-'90s, our design options were fairly limited. Heck, my first experience on the Web was on a text-based browser that provided me access to page upon glorious page of stark, blocky Courier. White text. Black background. 100% responsive.

When visual browsers finally hit the scene, ushering in images and the `font` element, we web designers finally had the opportunity to move out of monospace. I'll leave it to Jason to delve into the history of typography on the Web, but the advent of visual browsers opened the floodgates for use (and abuse) of type online. It was the desktop publishing revolution all over again: a direct assault on the sensibilities of anyone with even the slightest understanding of typography.

Over the years, we've made a lot of mistakes with web type: fonts embedded in images. Fonts embedded in Flash. Fonts embedded in JavaScript. Many of those were attempts to bypass the gridlock created by browser makers, type foundries, and the W3C, who couldn't come to a consensus on how to balance a desire for more type options on the Web while ensuring typographers got paid for all of their hard work. While they bickered, we soldiered on, looking for more accessible and maintainable ways to use more typefaces.

And while we were busy tinkering with sIFR and Cufón, eagerly awaiting the day we could abandon those hacks and have real browser support for actual font formats, an army of little black rectangles had caught a whiff of the awesome content we were serving up to desktop browsers.

Like ants at a Sunday picnic, these little black rectangles initially appeared one or two at a time. They were easily ignored, a nuisance. Nothing to take too seriously. But before we knew what was happening, that trickle turned into a flood and those little rectangles were hungry. Instead of taking a crumb here and there—which we tossed to them with a great sense of self-satisfaction—these ambitious ants were carrying off whole deli trays and the friggin' *New York Times*.

These little black rectangles are, of course, the surge of handheld (or at least hand-holdable) devices that have been redefining our concept of "the Web" almost daily. They exhibit widely variable screen sizes: from about the size of a matchbook, to ones that are bigger than an extra large pizza. They sport a plethora of pixel densities, new interaction methods, unpredictable network connection speeds, and low-powered processors that can't possibly compete with traditional laptop and desktop CPUs (not to mention a handful of different operating systems and browsers). All of these factors affect how—and even whether—your typographic choices will make it to your customers, and it's a lot to take in.

Thankfully, Jason has your back. The book you're now reading is invaluable: it's chock-full of useful approaches, practical code samples, and advice for dealing with typography in the age of responsive web design.

By the time you finish this brief book, you'll be ready to handle pretty much any device someone may throw at you. But hopefully they won't. Devices are hard. And expensive.

—Aaron Gustafson
Author, Adaptive Web Design

Preface

There are primarily three different but related audiences for this book:

- "Traditional" print-focused graphic designers
- Web designers
- Frontend developers

"Traditional" graphic designers need to know how to bring their knowledge of typography to the Web, how to find what's available, and how to use web fonts and understand technological limitations.

Web designers—many of whom don't have a traditional design education—need to understand the value of typography, what it can bring to their design, and what to watch out for when implementing web fonts.

Frontend developers are just as important: they're often handed the job of incorporating web fonts into the site and are expected to do so successfully. Putting that first line of JavaScript or CSS in place is easy. Making sure the best methods for embedding are used, ensuring fallbacks are in place and tuned, and getting the best performance takes knowledge, time, and a bit of persistence.

What You Need to Know

I've purposely kept the required technical knowledge modest in this book. In truth, you only need basic familiarity with HTML and CSS to make use of web fonts, though a smattering of JavaScript will do wonders to finesse the experience. All the sample code is complete and commented, so you may well be able to just take the sample code, work it into your own project, and modify it from there.

What You Don't Need to Know

All the code is kept fairly minimal, so while it will certainly make your life easier, you don't need to know anything about any CSS preprocessors like LESS or Sass. Likewise, the JavaScript is mostly cut-and-pasted from what the font services provide, to emulate what you are most likely to encounter when working with the font services on your own. It never hurts to know more, but I've tried to ensure that even relative beginners can still get the most out of the examples provided.

About the Examples

The example files have been tested in a wide variety of both desktop and mobile browsers, on several different platforms and OSes. While nothing is certain in life or web development (aside from death and taxes), I've done my best to be sure that the code provided will give consistent results wherever you use it. The text used is generally excerpts from *Moby Dick* by Herman Melville, a wonderful piece of literature that is also unencumbered by copyright. It makes for much more interesting samples than paragraphs of "Lorem Ipsum," to say nothing of how much more naturally it flows within the page.

Organization of This Book

This book is organized in two parts. Part I is focused primarily on some typography fundamentals, a brief history of the evolution of type on the web, and where typography fits in the design process. Part II is where we get into the details of implementation and the heart of what it means to make your typography responsive. While it may be tempting to jump right into the details, I do recommend at least skimming through Part I to make sure you don't miss some of the important aspects of "why" behind the large amounts of "how" in Part II.

Conventions Used in This Book

The following typographical conventions are used in this book:

Italic
> Indicates new terms, URLs, email addresses, filenames, and file extensions.

`Constant width`
> Used for program listings, as well as within paragraphs to refer to program elements such as variable or function names, databases, data types, environment variables, statements, and keywords.

`Constant width bold`
> Shows commands or other text that should be typed literally by the user.

Constant width italic

Shows text that should be replaced with user-supplied values or by values determined by context.

This element signifies a tip or suggestion.

This element signifies a general note.

This element indicates a warning or caution.

Sample Code Repository

I've started a repository on GitHub with the sample pages referenced in the book, in addition to the links provided (this repository will always have the most up-to-date code). You can find it here: *http://bit.ly/rt-code-repo*.

Using Code Examples

This book is here to help you get your job done. In general, you may use the code in this book in your programs and documentation. You do not need to contact us for permission unless you're reproducing a significant portion of the code. For example, writing a program that uses several chunks of code from this book does not require permission. Selling or distributing a CD-ROM of examples from O'Reilly books does require permission. Answering a question by citing this book and quoting example code does not require permission. Incorporating a significant amount of example code from this book into your product's documentation does require permission.

We appreciate, but do not require, attribution. An attribution usually includes the title, author, publisher, and ISBN. For example: "*Responsive Typography* by Jason Pamental (O'Reilly). Copyright 2014 Jason Pamental, 978-1-491-90709-2."

If you feel your use of code examples falls outside fair use or the permission given above, feel free to contact us at *permissions@oreilly.com*.

Safari® Books Online

Safari Books Online is an on-demand digital library that delivers expert content in both book and video form from the world's leading authors in technology and business.

Technology professionals, software developers, web designers, and business and creative professionals use Safari Books Online as their primary resource for research, problem solving, learning, and certification training.

Safari Books Online offers a range of plans and pricing for enterprise, government, education, and individuals.

Members have access to thousands of books, training videos, and prepublication manuscripts in one fully searchable database from publishers like O'Reilly Media, Prentice Hall Professional, Addison-Wesley Professional, Microsoft Press, Sams, Que, Peachpit Press, Focal Press, Cisco Press, John Wiley & Sons, Syngress, Morgan Kaufmann, IBM Redbooks, Packt, Adobe Press, FT Press, Apress, Manning, New Riders, McGraw-Hill, Jones & Bartlett, Course Technology, and hundreds more. For more information about Safari Books Online, please visit us online.

How to Contact Us

Please address comments and questions concerning this book to the publisher:

O'Reilly Media, Inc.
1005 Gravenstein Highway North
Sebastopol, CA 95472
800-998-9938 (in the United States or Canada)
707-829-0515 (international or local)
707-829-0104 (fax)

We have a web page for this book, where we list errata, examples, and any additional information. You can access this page at:

http://bit.ly/responsive_typography

To comment or ask technical questions about this book, send email to:

bookquestions@oreilly.com

For more information about our books, courses, conferences, and news, see our website at *http://www.oreilly.com*.

Find us on Facebook: *http://facebook.com/oreilly*

Follow us on Twitter: *http://twitter.com/oreillymedia*

Watch us on YouTube: *http://www.youtube.com/oreillymedia*

Acknowledgments

There are many people whom I need to thank for their help, encouragement, and input. Meghan Blanchette and Simon St. Laurent have been exceedingly patient, positive, and insightful editors. Before listing anyone else I have to mention three very good friends and cohorts here in Providence: Josh Clark, for believing I had something worth saying to the web community; Jen Robbins, whom I admire tremendously, for thinking that my typographic rants could fill a book and for introducing me to her O'Reilly family; and Coryndon Luxmoore: friend, cycling pal, cynic, and undying devotee of Arial. Probably set at 12px. Your faith has been fuel for my campaign against bad type on the Web. :)

I'd also like to thank these kind folks for their knowledge, inspiration, and passion for doing great things: Tim Brown, Jason Cranford Teague, Steve Fisher, Brad Frost, Aaron Gustafson, Allan Haley, Jeremy Keith, Jim Kidwell, Dan Mall, Ethan Marcotte, Eric Meyer, Dan Rose, Richard Rutter, Jason Santa Maria, Dan Rhatigan, Jonathan Stark, Elliot Jay Stocks, Dan Venditelli, Aarron Walter, Ken Woodworth, and Jeffrey Zeldman.

I'd also like to say a special thank you to John Giannopoulos, Ed Platz, and John Zsittnik for their amazing support, for being the first people to publish my writing about web fonts, and for generally being good friends and colleagues. A huge thank you again to Aaron Gustafson and Jen Robbins for their insightful reviews of my initial draft; they helped turn my ramblings into writing in more ways than I could imagine. Finally, I have to thank my parents and brother for inspiring me to teach (at least in my own way), and my wife Ellen and children Trevor and Phoebe for putting up with a lot of late nights, long stints away at conferences, and a near endless string of type-related puns. Your patience has perhaps been ill-rewarded, but is appreciated more than I could ever say.

Responsive Typography: An Introduction

Ever since I began studying graphic design I've loved type and typography. When real web fonts started to become available, particularly with the launch of Adobe Typekit in 2009, web design changed for me practically overnight. In truth, after over 15 years designing and developing for the web, it became fun again. Great typography and type-faces can bring so much to the design of a site that it's practically a whole new profession. But even with this quantum shift in what's possible in web design, there persists a lack of awareness and print resources to help designers and developers navigate the new landscape. This book is meant to change that.

When I started work on this book, my intent was to create a resource for designers and developers to help them implement web fonts effectively. I certainly intended to provide some typography basics and a bit of the history of type on the web, but that was about it. What's happened in the interim has led me to change focus a bit. My research and use of web fonts developed alongside my adoption and practice of Responsive Web Design (see the following sidebar), and after a time some significant similarities and relationships began to emerge.

Responsive Web Design in a Nutshell

Responsive Web Design (RWD) is a design and development methodology for creating websites that scale and adapt depending upon the size and capabilities of the device on which content is viewed. Content and design elements can reflow, navigation patterns can change, and images can be scaled to provide the best experience on all devices without utilizing separate sites or apps. This approach was defined and popularized by Ethan Marcotte in an article on A List Apart and in a subsequent book titled *Responsive Web Design* published by A Book Apart in 2011.

Ethan defined the basic concepts of RWD as including three main techniques: a fluid grid (rather than fixed-width), flexible media (that would scale with the rest of the page), and incorporating media queries to change the layout and flow based upon window or viewport size.

These ideas started to gel into something larger than the parts—so much so that I decided it really was worth giving it a name: *Responsive Typography*. While it may seem like a buzzword landgrab, I think there are some very important aspects to practicing good typography in the age of responsive design, so it really does warrant the name and the consideration.

In keeping with Ethan Marcotte's introduction of Responsive Web Design, I'm going to introduce the main tenets of good, responsive web typography as I see them—and then go into greater detail throughout the book. Truly responsive typography must be:

Performant

It's the Web, and it's our job to get the content to the user as fast as possible. Because type is a critical element of design, we have to find ways to deliver our design without compromising the delivery of the content:

- Load only what you need: include fonts with consideration, and only load the weights and variants you call for in your design.
- Choose the fastest way to serve your fonts: through a service or your own hosting infrastructure.
- Leverage techniques to get your content on screen—fast—by including CSS that doesn't use web fonts, and then swaps out for the web fonts once they're loaded (like a progressively loading graphic).

Progressive

Again, it's the Web: it should be inclusive and should follow the tenets of Progressive Enhancement. When properly implemented, 98% of the browsers used on the Web can load and render web fonts. *But 100% should load your design.* You can decide how best to implement this: lean toward "fallback-first" optimization, or assume the presence of JavaScript and tune for the smoothest transition:

- Use both JavaScript and CSS methods for web font loading when possible.
- Use "while the page is loading" CSS to speed both the rendering of content and its transition from "fallback-fast" to "@font-face polish."

Proportional

This was one of the most significant issues I've seen with typography when coupled with Responsive Web Design. It's not until the design starts to scale that you realize how important proportions are between headings and body type as screen sizes change:

- Basic default size should be left to the OS and device, but screen size should influence the proportions of headings and navigation.
- One scale does not serve all screens!

Polished

Design *is* the details, and great typography is no different. Don't stop with just getting the fonts on the page. Sweat the details; they're what get noticed:

- Use helpers like Typogrify and greater care in content entry to get the right glyphs (like proper quotation marks instead of vertical hashes).
- Tighten your letterspacing in headings. Loose letters look sloppy!
- Take advantage of ligatures, old-style figures, and fractions. Their use will really set your design apart. Browsers mostly support these special characters, and the fallback is generally harmless.

So there you have it: Performant, Progressive, Proportional, and Polished—the Four Ps of Responsive Typography. At least that's what has emerged so far! That's the fascinating part: it's not until we're on the journey that we find all the twists and turns in the road. But that also leads us to adventures we can't yet see, and that's all part of the fun!

I've spent the past several years working with various services, experimenting widely with self-hosting and fine-tuning, and have gathered and developed a number of techniques to ensure the successful implementation of web fonts—and good typography in general—across myriad desktop, tablet, and mobile environments. Altogether it becomes not just about typography, but about truly *responsive* typography that works and looks attractive and appropriate wherever it may be viewed. Now I'd like to put it all in one place so others can benefit from my endeavors. As I've become fond of saying: it's time to put Arial out to pasture.

PART I

A Bit of Backstory

Here we'll be covering a bit of typography basics, the history of web font formats, and where to put typography in the design process. If you'd rather skip straight to the nuts and bolts of it, head to Part II. But I hope you'll come back—there's a lot of the "why" behind the "how" explained here.

CHAPTER 1

On the Merits of Letters

Let's talk just a bit about typography, its history, and its impact on design. From the first written words, letters have been the vehicle through which meaning and knowledge have been conveyed. That job is performed in more than one way: the words the letters form impart meaning, *but the shape of the letters themselves* can make an important contribution.

First, a Few Terms Explained

While this book isn't meant as a complete stand-in for a true typography textbook, I'd be remiss if I didn't explain some of the key terms and concepts before we dive in:

Typography
> Quite simply, the theory and practice of selecting and setting type for printed or digital matter. In practice, it refers to typeface selection and setting the type for a given piece of content. Typography also ensures that the correct letterforms are used and proper punctuation marks are shown, generally finessing the final output to produce the highest-quality end result.

Typeface
> A specific design of letterforms, numerals, and punctuation that generally includes a complete set of letters, numbers, punctuation, and special characters of a specific weight or variant (such as Regular, Bold, Italic, etc.).

Typeface family
> A set of typefaces of a common design that includes a variety of weights and variants, often ranging from Light to Heavy in both standard and italic variants.

Font
> Technically, the font is the actual computer file that contains the information to define a single weight and variant of a typeface. For the purposes of this book, we'll

be focusing on the latter part of that definition: using the term to refer to *Trade Gothic Regular Italic* as opposed to that whole typeface family of Trade Gothic.

Serif
> The tiny "feet" and other little projections finishing of strokes of letterforms in typefaces such as Times New Roman or Georgia. Also used to refer to any typeface with those characteristics.

Sans-serif
> A typeface designed without any serifs (i.e., the strokes that comprise the letterform's end without any sort of projection).

Slab serif
> A serif typeface where the serifs themselves are generally the same thickness as the stroke weight of the letters themselves, which lends a somewhat chunkier feel to the typeface. Slab serif faces are often used for headings and display titles.

Terminals
> A term that refers to the ends of the strokes of letterforms. Some typefaces, such as Helvetica, have perfectly horizontal terminals in letterforms such as a lowercase "a" or "c" which tend to make them look more closed. Others have a slightly angled terminal, which can impart a more open feel and can aid legibility, especially at small sizes.

Words Have Meaning, but Letters Have Emotion

Consider the images conjured by the lettering on a stereotypical Chinese restaurant takeout menu, or a poster advertising an old Western movie, or the opening credits to the show *M*A*S*H* (see Figure 1-1). Or Apple's "Think different" campaign. Or picture any of the classic IBM ads, with their headlines set in those distinctively exaggerated thick-and-thin stroked letterforms. It's hard to use Bodoni without that coming to mind, at least in some subconscious way. That's pretty effective branding when a company can own an entire typeface in our collective consciousness.

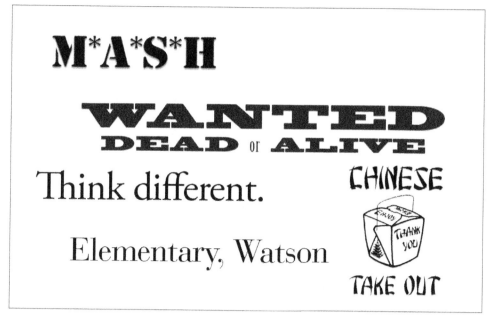

Figure 1-1. Our memory is filled with visual synonyms for brands—often defined by the type as much as the words

In design there are a few basic elements with which we have to play: composition, color, texture, shape, image, and type. When considering existing branding, color, style, and usability, why give up the one element that covers the biggest part of the page? Type can be as expressive or as utilitarian as you like, and the impression it makes is magnified by the fact that it's so often 90% of what you see on the screen or the page (at least in publications and websites). So let's leave the land of neutrality behind and really dive into our own expressiveness.

Type is wonderfully versatile and can convey far more than simply the content of the words it spells. It can have gender, color, tone, and emotion all its own. Good typography uses this to impart greater meaning. Great typography can elevate and amplify the message even further, creating its own tension, dynamism, and nuance far beyond the words themselves.

Even when the desire is a bit more practical, choice of typeface impacts readability as much as size and contrast. The actual media makes a difference as well. Newsprint, fine books, mobile phones, television screens, and laptops all present type differently—with widely varying degrees of detail. Choose the form of your letters poorly and your message will be lost and your brand forgotten.

Remember to Be Memorable

When nearly all the sites on the Web are using the same few typefaces (let's face it: the overwhelming majority specify Helvetica or Arial), it's noticeable when you use something different. Very noticeable. You can instantly change the tone of the page by shifting the headings and body copy into something just a little bit different. And different can mean memorable—and that kind of memorable can translate into more visits, more recommendations and more transactions.[1] When website visitors make judgments about a site's usability and value based on aesthetics, every decision you make about your design matters. A lot.

Do Good Looks Affect Usability?
You'd be surprised just how much they do. A good place to learn about the topic is this post by Jennifer Chen on Usability.gov (*http://bit.ly/rt-aesthetics*), titled "The Impact of Aesthetics on Attitudes Towards Websites."

Roots, Rhythm, and Rhyme

As with the examples at the beginning of the chapter, we know we associate certain letterforms with topics, places, and times. Those associations can be used to support (or contrast) the message of your design—but you can only do so if you understand and identify those associations. This is where knowing your history—your roots—and doing some research helps unearth details that really enrich your design. Identifying typefaces that have a relationship to your content or client can give a sense of place, evoke a mood or even reference a specific period in history.

I was fortunate to have been in Paris recently with my wife, and one of the things I sought out was one of the old Métropolitain signs for the Paris subway (originally designed by Hector Guimard). That typeface instantly transports you to not just the place, but that period of time, with its distinct relationship to the Art Nouveau style (see Figure 1-2). Interesting ties can be seen in other city transportation systems, like Helvetica in the New York City subway system or Johnston in the London Underground. But a single typeface is not the only consideration. More often than not, you will likely want to pair different typefaces together, and not every combination will sing in the same key.

---

1. As opposed to memorable like, "Hey, remember that legal services site we saw that used Comic Sans for their headings?"

Figure 1-2. Metro sign outside the Louvre in Paris

The pairing of typefaces and their impact on harmony and readability is a tremendously important aspect of design. Using a distinctive typeface in headers is great, but without considering what comes after, one can end up with some fairly odd bedfellows. The aforementioned Métropolitain typeface would look a bit odd sitting atop a few paragraphs of Helvetica or Arial, but Parisine (designed in the late 1990s and now the standard for use in the Paris Métro system) has a clear relationship and historical tie that might make a lot more sense. (Well, setting headlines in Métropolitain might not be the best choice for readability, but that's not the point here.)

What we want to achieve is a visual harmony that helps the reader flow from one element to the next, so pairing typefaces that have similar characteristics can create some wonderful and unique designs. Of course, you may choose to go in the opposite direction and look for pairings that have greater contrast in styles. There's no absolute "right way" —but that's the nature of design. Sometimes rules are meant to be broken, so long as the result feels right.

Adventures in Typeface Pairing

Here's an experiment you can try at home: when looking for a typeface for body copy to pair with one you've selected for headings, look at other typefaces from the same designer. Even when they aren't designed together, there are often relationships that stand out simply because they were drawn by the same hand. A personal favorite is headings set in Lubalin Graph—a great slab serif—and Avant Garde, the sans-serif that inspired it, for body copy (see Figure 1-3). The harmony created by the similarity in letterforms enforces a rhythm between heading and copy that flows elegantly from one to the other.

Queasy about Queequeg

He was going on with some wild reminiscences about his tomahawk-pipe, which, it seemed, had in its two uses both brained his foes and soothed his soul, when we were directly attracted to the sleeping rigger. The strong vapour now completely filling the contracted hole, it began to tell upon him. He breathed with a sort of muffledness; then seemed troubled in the nose; then revolved over once or twice; then sat up and rubbed his eyes.

Figure 1-3. Lubalin Graph paired with Avant Garde, both drawn by Herb Lubalin

When looking for pairings, it can also help to consider x-height (the height of lowercase letters compared to uppercase ones), overall horizontal scale (look at the width of letters set in Helvetica or Arial compared with Verdana: the latter is much wider and rounder), and stroke weight. In a rare bit of foreshadowing, I'll mention that you would do well to remember this trick when we get to later chapters on fine-tuning your fallback fonts and CSS. All of these characteristics come into play when trying to find balance and harmony in your design.

So what's the rhyme in your reason? To add to your design and your message, not simply convey it. I appreciate Swiss design, but can't get behind the philosophy that type's only job is to convey the meaning of the words it forms. Helvetica (and others, but it's an easy target) is an extremely clean, clear typeface that does a stellar job of telling you which subway station you are in on the map, but will never convey the sense of place and history in the tile mosaic on the wall of the Canal St. stop. It's like expecting a two-cheek-kiss in a greeting from a drill instructor.

I don't presume to be enough of an authority on typography to cover it all, but I feel it's important to give you the background and reasons why we should dive in and use web fonts now, even though the technology is still relatively young, and there are a fair number of tricks and workarounds necessary to use them well. It's worth the effort, as your site will stand apart in dramatic fashion when it's done elegantly and with finesse. Websites aren't much without text, and since you have to set it in something, you may as well set it well.

The Evolution of Type on the Web

When the graphical web first came about, there was actually no way to specify type at all. It was just something you could set as a preference in your browser. The only way to use a specific typeface on your site was to make a graphic of that word or phrase in an image editor, save it as a GIF or JPEG, and add it with an `<img>` tag (see Figure 1-4). Given that you had no idea if the rest of the type was going to be set in a serif or sans-serif typeface, it generally meant you had to keep your expectations pretty low. After a few years we saw the introduction of the `font` attribute added to our vernacular, allowing us to specify a series of fonts that would be called in order, and the first one present in the viewing user's system would be the one shown. This ushered in the Age of Arial.

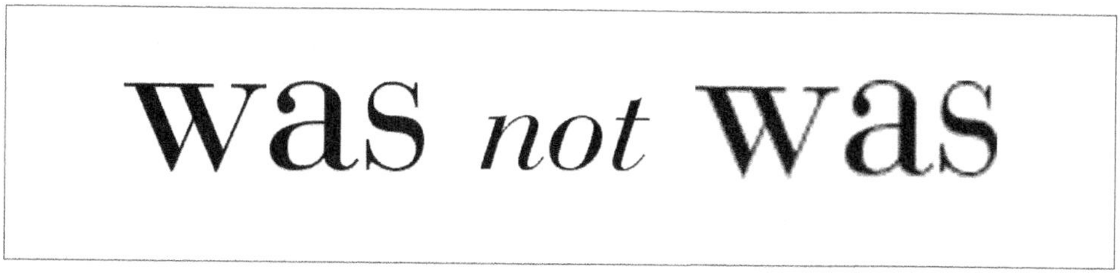

was *not* was

Figure 1-4. Pictures of a thousand words: for years we were forced to make graphics of words (right) rather than use live text (left) if we wanted a particular typeface in our designs

The only significant change here for a few years was the advent of CSS—though all this did was shift the specification of one of the few "web-safe" typeface choices from directly inline in the HTML to a separate style sheet. Microsoft was the first to support the new `@font-face` method of embedding web fonts for use on our sites, but due to incompatibilities with other browsers and licensing issues with font vendors, it was not successful at the time. Font replacement was the first "real" method for showing type "live" in a typeface other than one of the web-safe ones to come along, but with finicky and complex implementation, font replacement was often of limited use and was ultimately made obsolete by the next big development.

Finally, around 2007, `@font-face` made its mainstream debut, though font licensing remained a barrier to adoption until 2009, when the first web font service launched. Real typographic options for the Web—the *whole* Web—had finally arrived.

1990s–2007: The Angry Designer Years

The graphical web was first brought to us in the early '90s and along with the Mosaic web browser, began to usher in our modern browsing era. While it wasn't actually the first web browser, Mosaic was the first to support multiple platforms and enable viewing of images, listening to audio, and more. What it did not do was allow the specification of what font should be used to display the text on the page. It was entirely up to what the browser specified or the user preferred.

Helvetica Georgia

Times New Roman **Verdana**

Arial Lucida Bright

Figure 1-5. Our typographic vocabulary from roughly 1995 to 2009—sigh

We actually weren't able to specify any typeface at all until Netscape's introduction of the `<font>` tag in 1995 and its later inclusion in the HTML2 standard. As long as a typeface specified with the `<font>` tag was installed on the user's system, it would work. This is how we ended up with a list of fonts that were "web safe," meaning you could reasonably count on their presence on the majority of users' systems (a sampling of which can be seen in Figure 1-5). Because the new standard was designed with fallback in mind, you could list a series of fonts, and the browser would look through the list and display the content in whichever font was the first one found in that list. While some of the specifics changed, this remained the only "standards-based" approach available to web designers for over a decade.

 Remember this bit of foreshadowing: the idea of a list of fonts meant that content would come first, and the specifics of presentation were secondary. We must always remember to put "usable" before "perfect."

Not ones to leave well enough alone, web designers found their loophole quickly in the form of the GIF. Well, not necessarily a GIF, but when making a graphic of a word to use in a heading or a button, using the background transparency feature of the GIF format let us sit those lovely pixels nicely on our carefully tiled backgrounds. Naturally, during the design process those buttons would change about 37 times, requiring new graphics to be created, carefully exported, and then posted up to the web server for review. Things got even more exciting with the advent of mouseover states, so instead we could make 37 revisions of *two* graphics for every button and heading. That's your double rainbow right there. Not content to have that be all we had to worry about, accessibility for nonsighted users and the emerging prominence of search engines and their mysterious "bots" made sure we needed to have `alt` text for every graphic we so laboriously produced.

Lest I forget, we did have a significant upheaval in the web design industry with the introduction of Cascading Style Sheets (CSS) in 1996, with version 2 in 1998 supporting specifying `font-family` property. This allowed us to move our list of web-safe fonts from our markup to our style sheet. Remarkable progress. Not that it didn't bring many benefits, but it did nothing to really help push forward the cause of web typography until the inclusion of `@font-face` in CSS 2.1 in 2007. Sadly, `@font-face` would not become practically useful for another couple years.

A Step Sideways: Font-Replacement Techniques

Meanwhile, there were two other significant developments in the world of web-design typography, beginning in 2004. At that time, something called Scalable Inman Flash Replacement (sIFR) was released. Through a combination of Flash, JavaScript, HTML, and CSS, sIFR made it possible to use alternative fonts, which you created as Flash movies emedded on web pages. The displayed text could update dynamically, was still selectable, and overall made the Web a much better-looking neighborhood. However, it could be a bit tricky to set up and was not appropriate for all uses: you couldn't even really think about using it for body copy, and it was often very difficult to use even for navigation elements. Due to its reliance on Flash and JavaScript, it was clearly not a solution for the long haul, but it did provide the ability to utilize different fonts without running afoul of font vendors' licensing agreements.

A development a few years later was something called Cufón, which lashed together a generated font file, two rendering engines, and some chewing gum and baling wire (OK, guessing on those last two) to create another way of embedding fonts safely within your page without risking font piracy. Unfortunately the text was rendered nonselectable, so it was useless for nonsighted users or search engines. To its credit, though, it was easier to set up and more stable than sIFR, so it did become fairly widely adopted. Ironically, it came along just as things got a whole lot more interesting for very different reasons, sometime in 2009.

Finally: @font-face

Remember when I mentioned @font-face back in "The Evolution of Type on the Web" on page 9? The reason it sat around unloved except by a few for so long was due to the fact that while it was possible to include a typeface this way, and browsers were starting to support it widely, there were not many typefaces you could legally do this with, and you still needed a number of formats to make it all work. Licensing had always been what held back widespread adoption of web fonts, because there was no good way to prevent those fonts from being downloaded to a user's computer and then saved by him for use anywhere else. Finally, @font-face delivered a way to embed fonts in your page that browsers could keep from being downloaded, and with the launch of web font services came a way to manage that even better.

Admittedly, this has been a very brief overview. But that's so we can get to the good stuff.

May 27, 2009: T-Day

This was the launch date for Typekit, a new service that let users pick typefaces and easily add them to their websites with just a line or two of code. Behind that was @font-face and a crafty bit of wizardry that prevented users from saving those fonts to their own systems. More services launched soon after, with Fontdeck, Fonts.com, and WebINK being some of the first. I have to say that, more than any other advance or technology over the past decade, this is the one that put the fun back in web design for me.

Dawn of a New Design Paradigm

Alas, there is, of course, still more to this saga. We're not quite out of the woods just yet. So far we've been chatting primarily about desktop browsing—but many sites are reporting 15, 20, even 30% or more of their traffic coming from mobile devices (and one of my own client's sites routinely spikes to over 50% mobile traffic during high-traffic periods). In truth, the global trend is for the majority of traffic on the web to tip in favor of mobile within the next year. According to StatCounter (*http://bit.ly/rt-mobilestats*), in just the past year global web traffic from mobile devices has increased over 50% (see a few examples in Figure 1-6).

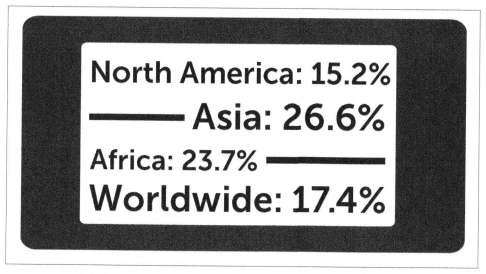

Figure 1-6. Global web traffic from mobile devices, with some data by continent as reported by Mashable in August 2013 (http://bit.ly/rt-mash)

So what about mobile devices? Well, there are over 50 typeface families available on current iOS devices, with some really nice choices. But we're still effectively stuck with the "lowest common denominator" choices if we want to be really consistent. And then there's Android: one of the most prevalent smartphone operating systems out there comes with—wait for it—three fonts. Well, actually four, as of the most recent release, Android 4.4. *Cue wails of despair and gnashing of teeth.* Clearly there is a need for a better solution to provide any sort of consistency and distinction across devices, platforms, and browsers.

Even though browser support is there for `@font-face`, font formats remain an issue. Thankfully the formats are available and we can safely and reliably serve our designs as intended to millions of mobile devices, as well.

Font Format Finagling: Who Shows What and Where

While adoption of `@font-face` was a big deal, there were and are still some significant technical issues with which to contend. First and foremost are file formats: in order to support the fullest range of browsers, OSes, and devices, one must support no fewer than four different file formats for every variant of every typeface! Only recently has a single format emerged as an agreed-upon standard for the future (I'll get to which one this is in a moment). It leverages elements of HTML5 and CSS3 to provide reasonable protection for font vendors, while evolving into a format and standard that can work and be supported across all devices, platforms, and operating systems (well, eventually —as of April 2014 about 77% of devices accessing the Web support it). However, with access to all of the file formats, fonts added with `@font-face` are viewable on over 90% of devices on the Web (when tablets and other mobile devices are considered alongside full-fledged computers, vendors such as Typekit and Fonts.com believe the number to be closer to 98%) (see Figure 1-7).

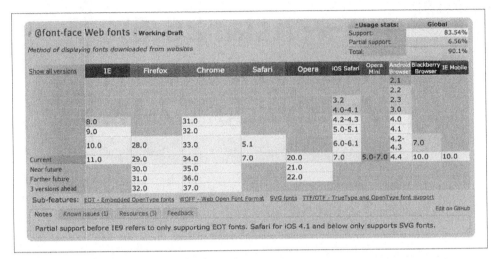

Figure 1-7. Browser support for `@font-face` as of May, 2014 from Caniuse.com

Let's dig a bit deeper into the issue of file formats. You'll have to bear with me just a little bit; this is going to get confusing. One of the most common desktop formats for fonts now is TrueType, although that is being supplanted by OpenType. While TrueType originated at Microsoft, Internet Explorer (IE) is just about the only browser that doesn't support it for use on the Web (though partial support came around with IE 9). If you want to support earlier versions of IE, you need to use the EOT (Embedded Open Type) format, but don't expect that to work anywhere else. That's two. If you want to support earlier versions of Safari (both desktop and mobile), SVG's your choice (that's Scalable Vector Graphics). That's format number three. And if you want to go with the "now just about a fully ratified standard" called WOFF (Web Open Font Format), well, that will do in almost all current browsers (finally including Android, as of the most recent 4.4 release). And just to be clear: none of it works in Opera Mini.

Opera Mini is the only modern browser that does not support `@font-face`. It's designed to be ruthlessly efficient with bandwidth and hardware resources, which is why it's used on many of the devices deployed in the fastest-growing markets in the world (which are also some of the most bandwidth-constrained). Asia, Africa, and India see significantly higher percentages of mobile traffic on Opera Mini than almost all other browsers. Bit of a bummer that it doesn't support nicer type.

Why all the formats? Why indeed. TrueType and its successor, OpenType, are the de facto standard on the desktop these days. OpenType supports all sorts of typographic goodness—such as full Unicode support for more than 65,000 glyphs, ligatures (think nicer glyphs for double characters like ff, as seen in Figure 1-8), and cross-platform font files—so there is no longer a need for separate Mac, Windows, and Unix file formats. What is lacking is any kind of protection native to the file format to limit use on the Web, like precluding a font file from being served from one domain and included for display on another. To counter that limitation, Microsoft came out with the EOT format as far back as 1996. However, IE was the only browser to ever support it.

Figure 1-8. Examples of ligatures (standard characters to the left, ligature glyphs to the right in each pair)

SVG is the third format, and while it is supported on a number of browsers, the only real reason we are discussing it is that prior to iOS 4.2, it was the only format supported on the iPhone. While that changed at the beginning of 2011, it's still a bit early to forget SVG entirely.[2]

---

2. As of June 2014, usage of those early versions of iOS seems to have dropped to about 1% of iOS devices globally, according to Caniuse.com (*http://bit.ly/rt-iosstats*), so it may well not be an issue for your user base.

Finally, there's WOFF. WOFF is the only font format to reach Recommendation status with the W3C, and it should be come an official standard soon. Technically, WOFF is essentially a wrapper for TrueType or OpenType fonts that adds a significant amount of compression (up to 40%), making it better suited for web use than other formats. As of this writing, more than 77% of devices on the Web can handle WOFF fonts, but there's still a ways to go before support can be considered universal and other formats can be dropped.

And So the Stage Is Set

So what does this mean for you, the web designer or developer tasked with adding this support? Well, if you are hosting the fonts yourself, it means you need all four formats for every weight and style you intend to use on your site. This is the only way to be sure your web fonts will be seen on all the devices used to visit your site (at least the ones that support @font-face).

Of course, it wouldn't be the Web if there weren't a catch. Just because a particular browser and OS supports web fonts, it doesn't mean it supports them well. Shockingly, the primary cause for this caveat involves Windows—Windows XP in particular—wherein there debuted a new font-smoothing technology called ClearType. I won't delve too deeply yet into just how much this may vex you, but suffice to say it will likely cause you some angst in the short term. At least there is a brighter shade of gloom on the horizon where font rendering in Windows is concerned: Windows 7+ and IE9+ handle web fonts together quite nicely. But let's look at the whole process of how fonts show up on our screens in the first place.

CHAPTER 2

Progressive Progress

Every good relationship starts with honest dialogue. So let's be truthful. Type (until very recently) was never intended for viewing on a computer screen. It was designed to be printed. Usually by inking metal and transferring it to paper. There is no such thing as "paper resolution" or "ink aliasing." In order to reproduce forms of letters as clearly and cleanly as ink on paper, a few, shall we say, quirks had to be overcome. As in life, all is not black and white when drawing letters on the screen. It is full of shades of gray—at least when it's done well. Those shades of gray (well, technically red, green, and blue) among the black help smooth edges so our eyes see a smooth curve rather than a blocky jagged edge. Over time, resolutions have become higher, screens crisper, and screen refreshes faster, but the basic problem hasn't changed. The eye must be fooled in order to make the reading experience anything like that of ink on paper.

As I've described, some issues exist that cause fonts to display slightly differently on one platform versus another. Resolution, sharpness, and density of pixels (the actual dots of color on the screen) all come into play, and they vary widely from one device to the next. But beyond that is actually how the fonts are drawn by the operating system on the screen in the first place. Mac and Windows have always had their differences (that's an understatement), even on something as fundamental as the number of pixels per inch on screen. The Mac held to 72 (mirroring the print convention of measuring type size in points, of which there are 72 per inch) and Windows stuck with 96. And neither really made any sense, because as screens got larger and resolutions increased, that measurement was never well-connected with reality.

A Concise History of Font Rendering

All the various font formats in use today are essentially formulas: combinations of curved and straight lines that form the shapes of letters with mathematical accuracy. The trouble is, those curves must translate to dots in order to be drawn. And when type sizes change, resolutions change, and pixel densities change, then the map of dots that corresponds to the curves defined in the font are different every single time (see Figure 2-1). Here is where the philosophical differences come in. In order to comprehend the full extent of our dilemma, it's necessary to understand the different approaches taken by Apple and Microsoft when it comes to font rendering, and just how different font files are from what is drawn on the screen.

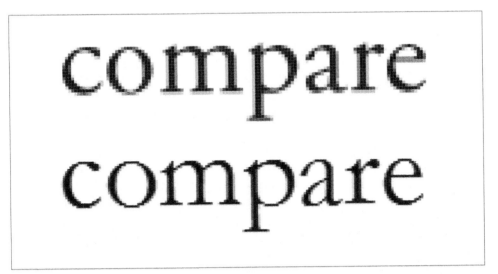

Figure 2-1. Close-up view of a word set in Garamond on MacOS (above) and Windows XP (below): note the hard baseline and flattened curves in the Windows XP version (even with ClearType enabled)

Apple uses *anti-aliasing* (grayscale dots between black and white) to smooth curves optically and has decided a little softness is acceptable in order to more closely approximate the typeface as it was originally designed (even if that sacrifices some sharpness). Interestingly, a large part of text looking natural and closer to the actual printed page comes from that very inaccuracy. It's much like listening to purely digital audio versus audio that comes from an analog source like a record or a cassette. There's a "fuzziness" and softening of the sound that blends things subtly, creating a more natural and less "man-made" sound in the process. Microsoft took a different approach and opted for clarity over accuracy, nudging the outlines of fonts over to the pixel grid in order to have type look sharper on screen, even if it loses some of the nuance of the original typeface design. With higher-quality screens, I suspect that there would be less eyestrain and fatigue from using an Apple device than one from Microsoft.

Font rendering in Windows has changed quite a bit over the years. Windows XP shipped with a text-rendering engine called GDI+ and a font-smoothing technology called ClearType. Unfortunately, when Windows XP shipped with this new marvel, it was off by default—and it was not that simple to switch it on. Later versions of Windows defaulted to *on*, as did versions of IE 7 and later. ClearType being on or off has had a huge impact on how text renders on screen, but unfortunately there is no way to know if it is on or off (from the website's perspective), so that leaves us with a bit of a dilemma. To confuse things further, Microsoft introduced a new and much improved text-rendering engine called DirectWrite with Windows Vista, continuing on in Windows 7 as well. This brought significant improvements, but it still differs from how Apple renders text, so we are still left with significant variation in appearance between platforms.

Apple's text rendering is driven by a technology called Core Text, which is the font-rendering engine behind both Mac OS X and iOS. Apple opts to stay truer to the font's design, which is why at small sizes the amount of subpixel work leaves type looking at times a bit blurry and soft (although at larger display sizes it is very sharp, smooth, and accurate). I would contend that most of the time that softness is not necessarily a bad thing, but that varies widely in the eye of the beholder. Technically, one of the biggest issues that accounts for this visual difference is that Core Text anti-aliases text in both directions: horizontally (x-axis) and vertically (y-axis), and GDI+ does not (which is the cause of much the marked jagginess of text in Windows XP, with ClearType or without). DirectWrite does anti-alias on the y-axis, but it enforces a cleanup along the baseline that tends to almost "clip" the bottom edge of some letterforms, subtly altering their balance. So how exactly do type designers handle these technical challenges and bring typefaces to all platforms successfully? I'll give you a hint.

Hinting: Crib Notes for Font Rendering

Although these differences are not an inherent problem, it is a problem that all the information necessary to tell Windows systems how to render fonts properly is not always present. Remember when I mentioned that fonts were never originally designed to look perfect on screen? This is where we run into trouble. The thing is, Windows needs a hint now and then on just how to render a given font. Those hints are actually part of the font file, but many older fonts simply don't contain the hints in the first place, as on-screen accuracy was not the primary concern. It should be noted that newer fonts generally contain hints, but that's a relatively small percentage of the more than 150,000 fonts in existence. Font vendors have been working furiously over the past few years to remedy this, but it is a very labor-intensive process that must be done by hand.

The problem with font rendering on screens is that screens are made up of grids of square pixels, and letterforms are made up primarily of curves. Round curves don't fit square grids any better than square pegs fit round holes. Somehow, the pixels need to be arranged so as to look optically more correct; then anti-aliasing can fill in the rest, and what we see more accurately reflects how the typeface was designed. Both Apple's Core Text and Windows' DirectWrite technologies do a good job of handling this sub-pixel landscape, but GDI+ does not. To make GDI+ fonts look better requires a talented "hinter" to manually examine every glyph and literally push pixels around by hand at various smaller sizes to get the best fidelity to the original design. Larger sizes have enough pixels in them to not require this level of attention, but common text sizes for body copy suffer greatly without it.

Some font vendors will let you know if their fonts are hinted or not, and most are working hard to bring that same level of finesse and polish to all of their offerings—but it's not an overnight kind of endeavor. It will likely take a bit of time to get there. In the meantime, it means that short of testing in an older Windows setup, you simply won't know. This can be tried in various "browser snapshot" services, but truthfully, the best way to discover rendering problems with typefaces is to set up a test system that will let you see for yourself. Virtual machine software like Parallels, VMWare Fusion, and Virtual Box allow you to run full virtual machines on your regular system, so you can test browsers and interaction, but these do require a fair amount of storage space for the virtual hard disk files. Either way—service or surrogate system—once you can see how things render, you can decide if the audience size warrants changing the font selection or possibly utilizing some other tricks to fool IE into doing a better job of smoothing fonts. Or just disable web fonts solely for Windows XP users (this is drastic and not 100% reliable, but it can be done, or so I hear). We'll get into more of those cases with some solutions to try later on in the book.

Now that you know how the fonts get drawn on screen, let's talk a bit about how and when they should come into your design process.

CHAPTER 3

Where Is Typography in the Design Process?

This question is nearly as old as the written letter. Or to put it more flippantly:

> Which came first, the Chicken or the "C", the "h," the "i," the other "c," the "k," the "e," and the "n"?

A popular cry recently has been for designers to design from the content out—sometimes with the variant "from the typography out"—in order to focus on creating the best presentation of the content itself. The theory being if you have a really well-designed piece of content and build a site design framework around that, you're always putting the most important element of the site—the content itself—at the forefront of your design efforts. While the purpose of this book isn't to focus on supporting or disputing this notion (and for the record, I think there's much merit here), it does highlight the importance of considering type very early in your design process. You can't design "content first" without type!

Beyond aesthetics, there's consideration of history (does the typeface relate to a certain point in time connected with the content, or have a historical connection to the brand, as in Figure 3-1?), the amount of copy to be set (smaller amounts can be set in a more expressive font; longer passages of body copy might warrant a more "workmanlike" selection), and whether that particular font is available as a web font (and how it looks on various device-and-OS combinations). Tragedy awaits those who don't check that last aspect and go all the way through the design process only to find out that a particular typeface is either not available for web use, or is but hasn't been hinted and renders so poorly on older versions of Windows as to be unusable.

Figure 3-1. Brilliant use of type to represent the New Yorker brand, even when no logo or other sign is visible on small screens

So where do you start? By reading (or writing!) the content itself. There's a reason why good designers don't like Lorem Ipsum. Lorem is a poser. Lorem is predictable. Lorem is, in short, not your content. The content itself should be what informs the design, and in the best of circumstances, the design can, in turn, inform the content (to a degree). They are (or at least should be) inseparable. And that process includes making choices about the typefaces to be used. If we were making design decisions based on Lorem Ipsum, we could all just install Trajan, center everything, and call it a day. But let's imagine that we have real content, that we've read it, we know who our client is, and we're ready to start designing. Now we have to make some choices based on the content with which we are working.

There Is No "Content First" Without Typography

First, we have to ask some questions:

- Is the content short or long?
- What is its intent: storytelling? advertising or marketing?
- Does the content have any clear cultural or historical connection?
- What do you know about the client?

The answers to these questions are all clues that can inform our typographic choices as much as ideas about color, composition, and imagery. Then we have to think about intent, relative importance, and context. There are lots of ways to convey importance or emotion beyond the words themselves; typeface choice, scale, weight, style, and color can have enormous impact. When designing for print, we know we can look through our own type catalogs or those of our favorite vendors, and if it fits, it'll do. But that's only part of the equation for web fonts, which is why we want to explore these options early and often, to ensure we make good choices that can actually be put into action. Not all typefaces are available for web use, with licensing that fits the budget site traffic levels and of sufficient quality to look good on all the screens our content is likely to encounter. Unless you consider these factors *before* you present the design to your client, all your work can be for naught.

A few more unexpected hiccups: what about weights and styles? Not all typefaces are available in bold or italics (VAG Rounded, I'm looking at you), and different fonts can have dramatically different file sizes (*ahem*, that would still be VAG Rounded to which I allude). In print it may not matter, but on the Web, every font must be downloaded, and some fonts can be 5 or even 10 times the size of an average Western one (typically between 30k and 40k). Yes, still referring to VAG (see Figure 3-2). Over 140k for a single weight (complete character set), with no available italics. Maybe this wouldn't be an issue for isolated use, but no matter how cool it looks in "book" weight for copy, telling your client that they can't put the book title or quotation in italics is likely to be an issue. Especially after it takes an extra 30 seconds to download before disappointing them anyway.

Figure 3-2. VAG Rounded, with it's rounded strokes, is a much larger file download due to the much greater number of curve points in the letterform design

Now that we've asked our questions and armed ourselves with knowledge of potential trouble spots, we can get on with designing. Here's where I have a bone to pick with the Swiss. Or more specifically, with those who subscribe to the "Swiss School" of design, which maintains that type should be utterly devoid of any emotion or style, that it should convey nothing more than the meaning of the words it spells out. I disagree—strongly.

As I mentioned in Chapter 1, we have a finite number of tools at our disposal in the design process. By removing any expressive qualities of the type we select, we remove the one design element that covers most of the page! Challenges are great, but meaning, emotion, and memorability are even better. A million web sites in Arial (or several million, more likely) makes Jack a dull boy. If your content is a story about a recent trip to Amsterdam, you might try something designed by Gerard Unger, like Praxis or the less-subtly named Hollander. Want to make it Spanish? How about Gans Ibarra—a beautiful and characteristic typeface that has loads of historical Iberian references.

Type choices can be obvious and decorative, like many from the Art Nouveau period (think those classic Paris Métro signs from Figure 1-2), or they can be just slightly different, like using News Gothic instead of Helvetica or Arial. News Gothic's slightly more open angling terminals (see definitions in Chapter 1) let the letters flow together a bit more smoothly and feel a bit more friendly. Need more inspiration? Check out this image from the Lost World's Fairs "El Dorado" page, designed by Naz Hamid (see Figure 3-3). It's a beautiful piece of work and does a great job evoking time, place, and even printing techniques.

Figure 3-3. El Dorado by Naz Hamid (http://bit.ly/rt-lost) from Lost World's Fairs

Once you've started making some preliminary choices, it's time to check availability, variety, and file size.

Availability

Not all typefaces you might have or come across are available to use on the Web. That's both from a technical perspective (i.e., the font formats themselves) and, arguably of greater import, from a legal one. Unless you're using a service or you specifically purchased a web-use license, you likely don't have permission to do so. Many font vendors and type foundries are offering web-use licenses these days, so even if you don't see one on their site, it pays to check with them and see. It's often a separate license you need to purchase, but generally rates are fairly reasonable. I'll talk more about that in the Chapter 4.

Variety (Is the Spice of Type)

If you're deciding on something for headers, you may not need multiple weights or styles —but don't forget that if you're specifying something for body copy (which I highly recommend), you're likely to need at least four weights and styles: regular (or book), italic (or oblique), bold, and bold italic. Since those are typically used when writing, you want to ensure that all the buttons in the content management system's (CMS's) editor will work as intended. This is where a designer I worked with once made a little misstep: she didn't realize there was no italic for a font she had specified for body copy. No go— time to find another typeface.

File Size

Likewise, it's worth checking file size, as you need to remember that users will have to download the sum total of all the fonts selected. Caching helps, but it does—if unchecked —introduce the potential for far more data traffic and performance penalty than you might realize. While there are no absolutes, in general each font (for Western character encodings like English) is between 20k and 40k, though that does vary widely. In general, the more complex the font, the larger the file size. For example, Trade Gothic Light from Fonts.com weighs in at about 22k; Edwardian Script Regular comes in at about 55k; and Fairbank Regular sits around 100k.

Now that you've got some history and fundamentals of typography down, let's look at just how to get them on screen in your project.

PART II

Getting Started with Web Fonts

Time to dig in to the nuts and bolts of implementing web fonts well, and take it beyond the basics to get really performant, progressive, proportional, and polished typography on your site.

CHAPTER 4

Buy or Borrow: The Designer's Dilemma

When it comes to actually utilizing `@font-face` to embed fonts on your site, you have some choices to make. Mainly, the choice is between self-hosting (where you serve the files along with the rest of your site) or using some sort of service. Each choice has its benefits, but there are some significant differences, so it pays to do your homework. Know what you want and what your project requires in terms of platform support, traffic levels, and typographic features, so you can be sure to make the right choice. It seems that most type vendors support one or both options these days, and even if you don't see pricing for the option you want on the website, it often pays to send an email and just ask. You may be surprised at the answer. Each of these options has a cost—material, qualitative, or both—so I'm going to explain how they work, what is involved in using them, and some of their pros and cons. As with everything else on the Web, it seems, the answer is a clear-cut "it depends," based on your individual circumstances and requirements.

First Things First: Weigh the Dollars and Sense

Let's get the money part out of the way. While there are certainly some notable exceptions, in most cases *good type costs money*. It costs because it's hard to design, hard to finesse, and hard to make work well on all platforms and in all browsers. So just as with photography, we should expect to pay something for its use.

As a fan of type, I enjoy having lots of options. But to make sure I keep having those options, there need to be type designers. And if I don't pay for fonts, there's no money to pay type designers. Multiply that by "everyone" and it's a pretty big problem. All those caveats and workarounds we have to contend with largely stem from the evolving landscape in font quality and typeface evolution, and if we don't actually pay the licensing costs, the companies working to smooth out the technical problems and make web fonts available won't survive, and our progress will stall.

Use with Caution!

A note about services that create web font files from your uploaded desktop fonts: plain and simple, it's probably a violation of your End User License Agreement (read about them in the following sidebar). Unless that EULA explicitly states you can use it for font embedding, it's not OK. (And realistically, the quality of an automatic conversion is likely to suffer.) It's a bit like a file-sharing network; the network itself may not be illegal, but what happens on it most certainly is.

Thankfully, the terms most of these services present are generally reasonable, and geared toward making it easy for small shops to get an account and start using them with all of their clients. Most self-hosting licenses and services base costs on traffic levels. This is why it's important to know your needs: while some services are only $100 per year for up to a million page views per month, if you have a much higher level of traffic, it can escalate costs quite a bit. One service shows a cost of $100 per month for 5 million monthly page views (a 12x increase in cost for a 5x increase in traffic). That may seem skewed, but the benefits in performance and reliability that come from using that service often can outweigh the cost.

EULA? (b)EULA?

End User License Agreements (or EULA, generally pronounced *yoo-lah*) are a standard thing in the software world: typically you are agreeing with one every time you use an app for the first time (you know, those "I Agree" buttons you click 37 times without reading anything). Fonts are in fact software, and all of them come with a EULA. Most say something to the effect that you will only use that font on the specified number of systems (usually five or fewer), that you won't redistribute it, and that you won't alter it in any way. Many have come to include more web-specific language, but the last part about altering it is likely the most relevant. Creating alternate file formats to use the font on the Web constitutes making an alteration (and then using it on the Web after doing so will likely violate web-specific language, as well), thereby in most cases violating the EULA. Since I'm not a lawyer, I'll let you look for yourself. Here are links to Monotype Imaging's EULA (*http://www.fonts.com/info/legal/eula/monotype-imaging*) and Hoefler & Co.'s EULA (*http://www.typography.com/home/eula.php*).

Now that we've covered the legal bits, let's dig in to the nuts and bolts of type families and files.

Type 101: A Font Is Not a Typeface

When getting started with using web fonts, it's important to point out the difference between a typeface and a font, and why that matters so much on the web. When talking about the two in this context, the typeface refers to the whole design, whereas font references the actual file containing the specific weight and variant of the typeface (see Figure 4-1). When specifying a font for inclusion on our site, we must remember that we are specifying a specific weight and style of that typeface rather than the whole family.

Figure 4-1. A font is not a face, but a face is made of many fonts

So for body copy we may be specifying Trade Gothic Regular, but for display use in headings we will likely want to specify Trade Gothic Bold, and if we want the `<i>` or `<em>` tag to be italic, we must include Trade Gothic Regular Italic. So when you are purchasing fonts for use on your site (or picking them in whichever service you have chosen) you must remember to include all the weights and styles that will be required (such as Book, Bold, Italic, and Bold Italic for body copy). Typekit and Google Web Fonts are the only web services (as far as I know at the time of this printing) that will automatically equate an available bold weight to a `<b>` or `<strong>` tag when used inside a block of copy that is set in one of their web fonts—though it should be noted that technically it's still a separate font file for each. While this does require a bit of extra work at times to set up, it also allows you to buy and embed only the weights and styles you need, ensuring that the total download for a site is as slim as it can be. (Fair warning: I will be stressing this point about download performance more than once!)

Browsers Are Not Type Designers!

Don't forget that you have to both specify the bold weight of the font *and* include `font-weight: normal` in your CSS. If you don't, you may end up with some browsers *double-bolding* your type. Firefox in particular is known to try to create "faux" bold and italic fonts, so if you are specifying things yourself, don't forget this step as it can produce some very odd-looking results.

Great. Now what do you do with this newfound knowledge? Move on to your next big decision: choose to do it yourself or use a service!

DIY: Self-Hosting

Self-hosting web fonts is not an overly complex affair; it just requires some basic attention to detail, a couple of important points with regard to structuring your CSS, and an understanding of the resources it requires (or conversely, how the limitations of your hosting environment can impact performance). Let's go through the basics of what files you need and how best to serve them.

Get the Right Assets

You have a few choices when hosting your own fonts: create them yourself; download open source ones such as Open Sans, Source Sans, Fira Sans, or others; or purchase them from a vendor that offers web-use licensing. Once you've acquired fonts for your project, you must include the font files for each weight and style (in the four formats discussed in Chapter 1: TT, EOT, SVG, and WOFF) on the server with the rest of your website files, and reference them using @font-face in your CSS.

 DIY Bonus!
One significant bonus when hosting yourself: you can group weights and variants in your @font-face declarations, so that standard tags will behave as they should without extra CSS (i.e., <b> and <strong> will be displayed with the specified bold weight without having to remap them in your styles—see the code in Example 5-1).

Serve Them Well

The next considerations are bandwidth and availability. If your site is hosted on a shared resource (such as the ones many of us use, from services like Media Temple, Bluehost, Rackspace, and others), the speed with which your fonts are served is only as fast as the rest of your site. Considering that the fonts may total 300k or more, even when some requests are cached on the user's system, that still adds a significant amount of traffic out of your monthly allocation. It also means that users from other geographic areas are loading all of the resources from your server, sometimes greatly increasing the load time if they are located in more far-flung locales (like reaching a US-hosted web site from Australia or New Zealand—often a much slower ordeal than you'd want to admit).

Keep Current

Finally, there is the subject of updates. I ask in all seriousness: when was the last time you downloaded an update for your fonts? I know that my answer until recently was

"What?" (even before getting to "Never"). But given the evolving nature of web fonts, the quality of hinting, and the emerging format standards, you can reasonably assume that this must become part of your regular maintenance.

Bandwidth, speed, and updates are all points to consider. With all that in mind, there are certainly cases in which self-hosting can be the smartest way to go, but let's look at the service option.

Something Borrowed (er, Rented): Using a Service

Web font services are the other option when it comes to `@font-face` usage. With these, you can sign up for an account (most offer some sort of free option), pick your typefaces, add a line of JavaScript or a CSS include, and either add selectors through the service or in your own CSS—and voilà: your fonts magically appear. Services are generally the easiest way to experiment with web fonts, and since most have some sort of free account, so it's easy to test the waters. Google has gone a step further and created its own web font service that is entirely free. One caveat with free and open source fonts such as those offered by Google is they may or may not have the same level of detail and polish as commercial offerings. Some certainly do, but many more may not.

The area where this will be most apparent is with hinting. It's quite a laborious process that requires a lot of experience and finesse, so it's the area most likely to be lacking. On the commercial side, all of the for-pay services have been updating fonts nearly continuously, making the process of staying current with the latest updates and technologies nearly seamless. I'll admit—I'm generally a big fan. As you can guess from the involvement of Adobe and Monotype, the industry is taking web fonts very seriously, and companies are investing heavily in improving the technology and quality of the fonts themselves.

There is, of course, more to the story. Font selection from services is pretty impressive, ranging from "merely" hundreds to over 30,000 available on Fonts.com, and even the smallest catalogs are full of high-quality fonts. (See a selection of the most common services in Table 4-1.) Searching for fonts on each of the sites is generally OK: with Fontdeck and Typekit have a couple of the more interesting ways of searching by tags, in addition to basic categorization like classification and foundry. I do appreciate the ability to search by designer, but only Fonts.com and Fontdeck allow that. Unfortunately, thus far no single source has created a truly comprehensive, easy-to-understand way to search. To be fair, that's not just a web font problem but a typeface search and selection conundrum in general.

Table 4-1. Some of the more common web font services

Service	Backed by	Embedding	Favorite feature
Cloud Typography	Hoefler & Co.	CSS	Fine control over included features
Fontdeck	Fontdeck	JavaScript & CSS	Robust tag-based searching

Service	Backed by	Embedding	Favorite feature
Fonts.com	Monotype	JavaScript & CSS	Search by designer
Google Fonts	Google	JavaScript & CSS	Free, very flexible use, including subsetting
Typekit	Adobe	JavaScript	Very visual search cues
Webtype	The Font Bureau	CSS	Search by intended size

Once you've selected the fonts you want to use, there is generally a choice to assign fonts to selectors through the service or set them up in your own CSS. I generally opt for my own CSS, as it affords more control over usage, font stacks, and fallback finessing. It also keeps the control over how typefaces are specified in one place (and in the hands of the designer).

Another benefit of using a service is bandwidth and availability. All of the major services use content distribution networks (CDNs) to serve copies of font files from geographic locations around the world, using address lookup techniques to serve files to users from the closest locations for the fastest response times. This has two important additional advantages: the services are redundant so that no single outage will prevent them from loading, and it drastically reduces the bandwidth and load on your own server.

So undoubtedly you're wondering about the catch. Here it is: traffic. The for-pay services all charge by page views per month. Generally those limits are fairly high (anywhere from 25,000 per month for a typical free account to one million page views per month on more "standard" professional accounts). This will work for many sites but, obviously, not all. All offer higher tiers of traffic, ranging up to 50 million page views per month or more, but for some the economics tilt toward using their own fonts and infrastructure, saving money in the long run. If the licensing you have allows for it, self-hosting may be more cost-effective, but that's a big if in many cases.

Now that you've learned the ins and outs of both hosting and services, we can get to the fun part: getting fonts on your site! There are still a few differences in the how of either choice, but for the most part the next steps are the same for both.

CHAPTER 5

Performance: Get Fonts on Your Site, Fast

After all you've read so far about the various methods at your disposal to add web fonts to your site, it's time to make a choice. Your next steps will be determined by which option you choose: self-host or service. I'll show examples for both options, most of which work in a very similar way, though with some important differences.

Self-Hosting

If you have a license that permits hosting yourself, or if it's a font of your own creation, you may end up deciding to follow this route. It may also make sense based on your users and network: if you have very high volumes of traffic and/or your own optimized CDN, you might save considerable cost with self-hosting. The initial setup is relatively straightforward, but there are a few gotchas related to the syntax used in setting up the @font-face declaration, so it will save you some headaches to keep a few things in mind. Have a look at the code in Example 5-1 and then we'll examine the parts and special considerations.

Example 5-1. Example @font-face declaration

```
@font-face {
  font-family: 'OpenSans'; ❶
  src: url('/fonts/OpenSans-Regular-webfont.eot'); ❷
  src: url('/fonts/OpenSans-Regular-webfont.eot') format('embedded-opentype'),
    url('/fonts/OpenSans-Regular-webfont.woff') format('woff'),
    url('/fonts/OpenSans-Regular-webfont.ttf') format('truetype'),
    url('/fonts/OpenSans-Regular-webfont.svg') format('svg');
  font-weight: normal; ❸
  font-style: normal; ❹
}
@font-face {
  font-family: 'OpenSans';
  src: url('/fonts/OpenSans-Bold-webfont.eot');
  src: url('/fonts/OpenSans-Bold-webfont.eot') format('embedded-opentype'),
```

```
    url('/fonts/OpenSans-Bold-webfont.woff') format('woff'),
    url('/fonts/OpenSans-Bold-webfont.ttf') format('truetype'),
    url('/fonts/OpenSans-Bold-webfont.svg') format('svg');
  font-weight: bold;
  font-style: normal;
}
@font-face {
  font-family: 'OpenSans';
  src: url('/fonts/OpenSans-Italic-webfont.eot');
  src: url('/fonts/OpenSans-Italic-webfont.eot') format('embedded-opentype'),
    url('/fonts/OpenSans-Italic-webfont.woff') format('woff'),
    url('/fonts/OpenSans-Italic-webfont.ttf') format('truetype'),
    url('/fonts/OpenSans-Italic-webfont.svg') format('svg');
  font-weight: normal;
  font-style: italic;
}
@font-face {
  font-family: 'OpenSans';
  src: url('/fonts/OpenSans-BoldItalic-webfont.eot');
  src: url('/fonts/OpenSans-BoldItalic-webfont.eot') format('embedded-opentype'),
    url('/fonts/OpenSans-BoldItalic-webfont.woff') format('woff'),
    url('/fonts/OpenSans-BoldItalic-webfont.ttf') format('truetype'),
    url('/fonts/OpenSans-BoldItalic-webfont.svg') format('svg');
  font-weight: bold;
  font-style: italic;
}
@font-face {
  font-family: 'OpenSans';
  src: url('/fonts/OpenSans-ExtraBold-webfont.eot');
  src: url('/fonts/OpenSans-ExtraBold-webfont.eot') format('embedded-opentype'),
    url('/fonts/OpenSans-ExtraBold-webfont.woff') format('woff'),
    url('/fonts/OpenSans-ExtraBold-webfont.ttf') format('truetype'),
    url('/fonts/OpenSans-ExtraBold-webfont.svg') format('svg');
  font-weight: 800;
  font-style: normal;
}
```

❶ This is whatever you want to use as a font family name in your CSS

❷ These lines list each of the file formats in a specific order that helps users avoid unnecessary downloads

❸ This is how you map to a specific weight, such as *bold* or *500*

❹ This is how you map to an italic style

Once this is in your CSS, you can reference that font anywhere you specify `font-family`, as shown in Example 5-2.

Example 5-2. Using the embedded fonts

```
body {
  font-family: 'OpenSans';
}
```

In general, there are two main parts to setting up web fonts yourself. The first part (the @font-face stanza) links to the font files and groups them into a font-family you can reference. The second part is just as you would reference any font-family in styling your site. Nothing fancy there, and by grouping the weights and variants by name, there's no need to add specific CSS to accommodate bold and italic fonts and styles.

Gotchas

- Be sure to use syntax in the url() that either starts from the web root with a leading / or http://—some browser versions won't load the fonts if you use relative syntax like ../fonts when referencing a location at the same directory level as a folder of CSS files. Some older versions of Firefox and IE in particular can be troublesome, but it's worth experimenting to see if you can use the more flexible relative format. Also note that Firefox can be particularly picky about where the fonts are served: it's generally best to try and keep them hosted and served from the same URL as the rest of your site.

- When you're adding the declarations to your CSS, you'll also want to list the font files in the correct order (as shown) so that the right browser will find the right files, ensuring the best performance on all platforms and OSes. This post from Paul Irish may be an older reference, but it's still quite valid: *http://bit.ly/rt-fontlistorder*.

- Also be sure to leave in @font-face declarations only for fonts you're actively using, or you'll be burdening your users with unnecessary downloads.

Bonus

Did you notice we've included font-weight and font-style? This is one of the nice benefits to hosting yourself. You can map each weight and style to a specific attribute value, simplifying the CSS you have to write and ensuring that standard HTML tags will render as expected.

Add the Performance and Progression Flair

I'll go into greater detail about what the Google Web Font Loader is in a moment, but for completeness I wanted to include the way to use it with your self-hosted fonts here (Example 5-3).

Example 5-3. Google Web Font Loader syntax for self-hosting

```
WebFontConfig = {
  custom: {
    families: ['OpenSans', 'My Other Font'],
    urls: ['/css/fonts.css']
  }
};
```

The families correspond to how you name fonts in your @font-face declarations, and the url of that CSS file must be referenced from your web root.

That's pretty much all there is to it—until you start to worry about all the other bits to really finesse things. I'll cover some examples of usage that apply to both self-hosting and services in just a little bit.

Using a Service

There are many really great web font services out there, and I'll go through a number of them later in the book—but for now let's start with a free one you can play with: Google Web Fonts. First you have to select some fonts, grab the code to link the CSS, and paste it into the head of your page (see Example 5-4 and Example 5-5). Then, you're ready to add the font families and use the fonts in your CSS. As with self-hosted fonts, be careful to add only the fonts you need. It's easy to forget, as you may often include more weights and variants during the design process in order to evaluate which works best in the browser.

Example 5-4. Google Web Fonts syntax for linking CSS

```
<link href='http://fonts.googleapis.com/css?family=Open+Sans:400italic,700italic,
        400,700' rel='stylesheet' type='text/css'>
```

Example 5-5. Google Web Fonts syntax for linking with JavaScript (plus Web Font Loader) with CSS fallback

```
<script type="text/javascript">
  WebFontConfig = {
    google: { families: [ 'Open+Sans:400italic,700italic,400,700:latin' ] }
  };
  (function() {
    var wf = document.createElement('script');
    wf.src = ('https:' == document.location.protocol ? 'https' : 'http') +
      '://ajax.googleapis.com/ajax/libs/webfont/1/webfont.js';
    wf.type = 'text/javascript';
    wf.async = 'true';
    var s = document.getElementsByTagName('script')[0];
    s.parentNode.insertBefore(wf, s);
  })();
</script>
<noscript>
```

```
    <link href='http://fonts.googleapis.com/css?family=Open+Sans:400italic,700italic,
          400,700' rel='stylesheet' type='text/css'>
</noscript>
```

In keeping with best practices on the Web, I generally recommend using both a JavaScript- and a CSS-based method for embedding the web fonts from a service. To the best of my knowledge, Fontdeck, Fonts.com, and Google Web Fonts are the only ones that give you both options straight away, and Typekit is the only one that will allow JavaScript only. But all the other services give you a link to a CSS file, which can be used with JavaScript anyway, courtesy of the Google Web Font Loader (see "Google Web Font Loader" on page 39).

There are plenty of reasons why you might use a service rather than hosting yourself. One of them is availability: not all fonts are available for self-hosting, and conversely, not all are available for use through a service. Chances are, though, that with literally tens of thousands available from a variety of sources, the font you need is available through a service. And by using those services, you get some serious performance horsepower behind your site.

All of the major services use CDNs to help serve font assets geographically closer to users requesting them, saving valuable load time. They also spend huge amounts of time and money researching and improving rendering across platforms and devices and are continually pushing out improvements to both their services and their fonts. This last bit is no small issue: without all of the effort put into manually hinting fonts to work well on Windows, we'd be leaving a lot of users stranded on the jagged peaks of poorly rendered letterforms.

No matter which method you use, there will always be the requirement to download font assets and render them in the browser. The speed of this will likewise always vary (it is the Internet, you know), so let's look at how we can incorporate a tool that will help us even out the experience: the Google Web Font Loader.

Google Web Font Loader

Initially launched in 2010, the Google Web Font Loader was developed in conjunction with Typekit, and was made an open source project that is now hosted on Github. Created to help deal with FOUT (Flash of Unstyled Text), the purpose is to provide classes injected into the HTML element of your page in order to be aware of the web fonts' loading state. Classes are injected for each font, plus an overall `.wf-inactive` or `.wf-active` class. As you might expect, the `.wf-inactive` class is injected on page load, and it's swapped out for `.wf-active` once all the fonts are loaded.

While this may not technically make the loading of web fonts faster, it serves a critical purpose in making the web page *draw* faster by a) enabling web fonts to load asynchronously to avoid blocking page rendering and b) allowing us to craft CSS targeted specifically at the fonts present during the load process to make the page *seem* to load faster. Sometimes perception is half the battle, and every second counts! In fact, according to Innovation Insights from Wired (*http://bit.ly/rt-fiveseconds*), 74% of mobile users will leave your site if it doesn't load within 5 seconds.

Typekit already uses the Web Font Loader by default, but you can use it with Google Web Fonts or just about any other web font service. There are a bunch of samples on the project page on GitHub (*http://bit.ly/rt-wfload*).

Let's break down the aforementioned JavaScript example:

```
<script type="text/javascript">
  WebFontConfig = {
    google: { families: [ 'Open+Sans:400italic,700italic,400,700:latin' ] }
  };
```

Here are the specific fonts, weights, and variants to be loaded:

```
(function() {
  var wf = document.createElement('script');
  wf.src = ('https:' == document.location.protocol ? 'https' : 'http') +
    '://ajax.googleapis.com/ajax/libs/webfont/1/webfont.js';
  wf.type = 'text/javascript';
```

The function ensures that the web fonts will be loaded with the same protocol (http or https) as the rest of the page:

```
  wf.async = 'true';
```

By specifying async=*true*, we specify to load the fonts asynchronously, ensuring we don't block the page rendering during the font-loading process.

Several other services offer some sort of asynchronous loading script; you just may have to hunt around a bit to find it:

```
  var s = document.getElementsByTagName('script')[0];
  s.parentNode.insertBefore(wf, s);
})();
</script>
```

This code snippet wraps up the JavaScript-loading script:

```
<noscript>
  <link href='http://fonts.googleapis.com/css?family=Roboto+Slab:700|Roboto:
  400,400italic,700italic,700' rel='stylesheet' type='text/css'>
</noscript>
```

By including this noscript block, we ensure that if JavaScript doesn't load, the user will still get the web fonts, even if it's without the loading classes.

Even Faster: Load Only the Letters You Use

The next logical step in optimizing performance is to load only the letters you need—but that only works if you know in advance what they are! It's been done quite a bit with icon fonts, where it's far more likely that you'd know exactly which ones you need (see "Icon Fonts" on page 74 for more details). Google Web Fonts does allow you to subset what is being embedded in the page, but this comes at a cost: if you optimize for just what's used on screen at the moment, you ensure that this download will work only for this specific page (or set of pages, if it's navigation or some other reused component).

In the age of CMSes, this can prove a difficult strategy to follow. Even if you were to sort out generating a character subset dynamically, you'd be losing the benefit of caching the font downloads, requiring a new download on every page. Even if it's smaller each time, the overall benefit may not outweigh the increased cost in HTTP requests and downloads.

That said, there may be situations where this is appropriate (such as using a specific font for a tagline or logo, or for more static navigation). The only two services I know that allow you to do this yourself are Google Web Fonts (*http://bit.ly/rt-gwfsubset*) and Hoefler & Co. (see *Custom Character Set* (*http://bit.ly/rt-hcsubset*)).

Here is an instance where subsetting is truly critical: non-Western character sets like Arabic, or typical double-byte fonts for Japanese, Chinese, Korean, and other Asian languages. In these cases, subsetting on the fly is not a luxury; it's a requirement. A typical double-byte font for a Japanese-language page could be 2.5MB (as opposed to 30k to 40k), containing over 10,000 glyphs! (See Figure 5-1.)

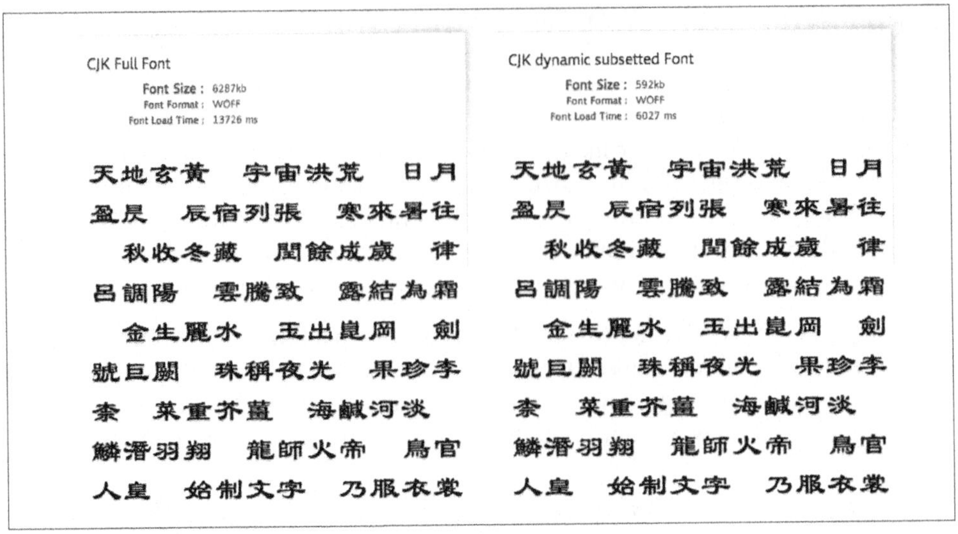

Figure 5-1. An example of Fonts.com's dynamic subsetting of some Japanese text: over 90% file size savings and 50% reduction in download time

Short of dynamic subsetting, it's nearly impossible to use web fonts without placing too high a burden on the user. To the best of my knowledge, Fonts.com is the only service that can do this, so keep that in mind when researching typefaces to use in your next Asian-language project.

Connecting Performant with Progressive

At the beginning of the book, I mentioned four key aspects of Responsive Typography. This is the first: Performance. Following the advice mentioned earlier, we can ensure that pages can load quickly because we're making sure to load only what we're using in our design, and we are loading them in a way that does not impede loading the rest of the page. The other part of performance is getting the content on the screen—fast. We'll talk about what prevents that—and what we can do about it—in the next chapter.

CHAPTER 6

Be Progressive: Font Sizing and FOUT

In this chapter we're going to talk about two important aspects of being responsive with your type: sizing it appropriately and getting it on screen fast. While we covered *absolute speed* in the last chapter, in this one we're going to tackle *perceived* speed, which ultimately may be more important. We'll also look at a key aspect of the notion of Progressive Enhancement. Essentially, it's planning for failure. You must design and code your site with the assumption that there will always be *some* point during the loading process or viewing experience when web fonts will not be present—and handling that appropriately is essential. By designing and developing for the brief moments before web fonts load, you're also addressing the (potentially) millions of visitors to your site for whom web fonts won't load at all (i.e., those browsing via Opera Mini).[1]

Code Sample

Download the source code to follow along and try this yourself.

View demo: *http://bit.ly/rt-demo-fout*

Download code: *http://bit.ly/rt-code-fout*

On Units of Measure

There are lots of choices in sizing type, but if you're looking to be most compatible with modern web design and development techniques, a relative unit of measure is extremely

---

[1]. I repeat this not to beat up on the Opera Mini team, but to stress that it's the Web; we just don't know what will or will not work tomorrow. To quote Jeremy Keith: "The best way to be future friendly is to be backwards compatible."

important. Rather than using a fixed unit of measure (px), you'll want to use em or rem (cleverly meaning a *relative em*).

I tend to stick with ems because if you base your text sizes, vertical margins and padding, and media query breakpoints all in ems, everything will scale uniformly. It's also crucial when dealing with high-resolution/high-pixel-density screens. Currently, these devices report more "standard" resolutions (like 320px wide on most phones), but if they report true resolution instead (as indeed some Samsung touch-screen laptops do as of this writing) then pixel-based sizing and breakpoints will be tiny and appear in the middle of the screen, rather than filling it as you'd expect.

This is specifically because each device manufacturer decides how text sized at 100% should render in order to yield what we expect as equivalent to 16px on the desktop. And since we've based our font size and breakpoints on 1em —a relative measure equivalent to 100% of that default size—our design will render as expected even on these kinds of systems.

The challenge with using ems is that they are relative to the parent of the object or entity in question. So if the <html> element is set to 100%, <body> copy is set to 1em, and <p> is set to 1em, <p> text would render (as expected) at 16px. But if you applied font-size: 1.25em to <body>, <p> would now render at 20px, or 1.25 times the 100% size. In order to get <p> to render at 16px, you would need to apply font-size: 0.8em to the <p>. It can make your brain hurt quite quickly.

However, there is a really simple fix: *don't apply font-size to containers*. Only apply it to elements of text themselves (i.e., the <h2>, the <p>, or to any class which is used on one of those text elements). If you stick to that rule of thumb, sizing in ems is generally quite easy to manage. And it's supported in every browser.

The rem attribute is another variant of relative measure that has become popular of late, as it gets around the font-size gymnastics by always referencing the root of the document to figure out what it should be. But it's not supported without adding another JavaScript polyfill in IE 8 or earlier. And while it's become something of the fashion to ignore those browsers, the unfortunate truth is that there are still many, many users browsing with that particular version. Globally, as of this writing, about one in five (via WinBeta.org (*http://bit.ly/rt-ie8stats*)).

Every site is different, but imagine turning one of five customers away at the door. Not many business owners would make that choice—especially when it's so easy to avoid. As I suggested, just don't specify text size for the container, and you can use ems with relative ease.

FOUT Is Our Fault

The dreaded FOUT, or Flash of Unstyled Text, is an unfortunately familiar trait of sites using web fonts. It's actually one of two possible scenarios: FOUT, arising from the content being loaded in a fallback font and then *snapping* into the web font once it loads (often reflowing the text in the process, making for a very jumpy experience), or worse, and sadly more common, you don't see anything at all except some random underlines (see Figure 6-1). Browser vendors seem to be rallying around the unfortunate practice of hiding the content until the web font loads (often set to a three-second delay).

This is the wrong approach, and is harmful to the adoption of web fonts in general.

The answer isn't, as some developers have called for, to not use web fonts at all, but rather to do our job and control the process with the tools we have at hand. Type is simply too important a design element to give up just because we're lazy. So let's look at this more closely.

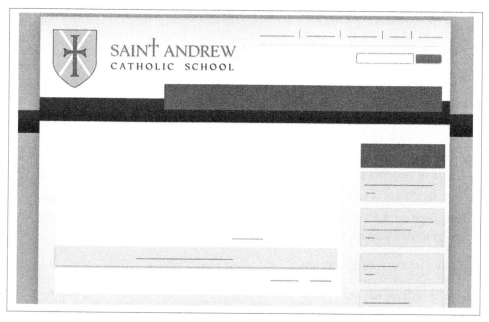

Figure 6-1. Flash of Unstyled Nothing - the all too common loading experience

FOUT is familiar, and it's put many people off using web fonts at all. It's also unfortunate in that it's largely preventable. (OK, there are some caveats, but it doesn't sound as dramatic with air quotes around it.) The key aspect that *is* preventable is the "Unstyled" part. Since we know we have the Google Web Font Loader-supplied classes (or the slightly different ones that Fonts.com supplies), there's no reason we can't style the fonts during the loading process and call only web-safe fonts as long as the loading class is present. This ensures we get content on the screen right away that can be tuned to minimize the difference between fallback and fully loaded.

We have to remember: it's not the fact that it changes from fallback to web font, but the *perception* of change that users notice. By styling the fallbacks to more closely match the spacing, word wrap, and flow of the fully loaded design, we can reduce the perception of change so it's almost unnoticeable.

Tuning Up Your Fallback CSS

As we discussed in "Google Web Font Loader" on page 39, when using Web Font Loader (or something like it) we have loading classes to work: those little gems wf-loading and wf-loaded. With these we can customize our CSS to have specific "fallback font stacks" set up that don't call web fonts at all during the loading process. By utilizing basic, well-supported CSS attributes like font-size, line-height, and letter-spacing, we can customize and tweak our fallback CSS to minimize or even eliminate any jump in size or reflowing of text during the loading process.

Ensuring that the text is drawn on screen right away and then transitioning smoothly to the rendered web font reduces the visible differences between the loading and loaded states, so the user notices the change far less. This greatly enhances the *perception* of speed. We'll look at the code in a bit, but first let's review what happens when a page is requested, how it loads, and where the pitfalls occur:

1. A user requests a page from your site
2. The page begins to load, including a reference to a JavaScript file to embed the fonts. One of two things happens when the script loads:
   a. JavaScript is enabled, so the script runs, *or*
   b. JavaScript is not enabled, so nothing more happens (unless you have cleverly inserted something in a <noscript> block, as follows)

Next, one of three things occurs:

- If JavaScript has run, fonts are loading and font events are firing, meaning CSS classes such as wf-inactive are being inserted dynamically into your page. You, as the clever designer and/or developer you are, have added to your CSS classes and declarations to help ensure that your text is rendering well both during and after the loading occurs.

- If JavaScript has not run but you are indeed clever, the <noscript> block containing a link to a CSS file is taking care of loading your fonts. While no font events will help mitigate display oddities during the loading process, in a moment or two all will be loaded and displaying according to your design.

- If JavaScript has not run but you have not included the `<noscript>` block, while no kittens will be harmed, you will have doomed your users to a far more pedestrian experience likely filled with poorly letter-spaced text set in Arial. You can do better!

Now, in the sequence of events just described, you'll notice that not only have we accounted for fallbacks should the fonts not load, but we've even created a fallback scenario for JavaScript not functioning and added a link to CSS that will load the fonts anyway. Very clever indeed. Your mother would be proud. (Unless you have fallen into that last case, but you still have time to redeem yourself!)

Before we dive into the code, let's take a moment to more clearly explain why we're taking the trouble to go through this exercise. Without trying to be flippant, it's important to point out that fonts differ from each other in more ways than simple appearance. Spacing can vary widely, which is why I recommend selecting fallback fonts that more closely match the horizontal scale of your chosen web fonts as much as possible. (For example, the Helvetica and Verdana typefaces vary greatly in width, so choose the one that's closer to your intent. For a comparison, see Figure 6-2.)

The quick brown fox jumpec
(Verdana)

The quick brown fox jumped ove
(Helvetica)

Figure 6-2. A comparison of Verdana and Helvetica showing significant differences in both overall width and the height of lowercase letters (x-height)

The problem you'll find is that while the web fonts are loading, either no text will display at all or it will show in the fallback font and probably reflow your text quite a bit (see Figure 6-4). This is exaggerated further when the web font selected is drastically different in size. This will cause a jarring reflow of the page once the web fonts load fully and the browser updates the user's window with the re-rendered page.

By using font events to introduce new CSS written specifically to address the display of the fallback fonts, we can adjust with the CSS `letter-spacing` and `font-size` declarations to minimize, or even eliminate, the reflow of text on the page. There is also the nascent declaration of `font-size-adjust`, but it's very unevenly implemented as of yet. This property attempts to instruct the browser how to scale the fallback font to more closely match the intended web font.

For our demonstration I've selected a lovely passage from *Moby Dick*—a tremendous work which also happens to be unencumbered by copyright restriction. We'll be using a simple pairing of Roboto and Roboto Slab for our demonstration, as they are open source, and therefore easier for me to ensure you have everything you need to work locally as we go (see Figure 6-3).

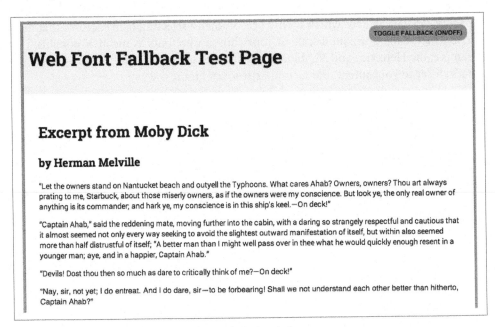

Figure 6-3. Sample page with web fonts fully loaded

This is where we'll start to get into the sample code. To fully prepare ourselves, we'll have to set up our page to use the Web Font Loader whenever JavaScript is enabled. It's worth noting here that the following code must be present on all the pages of your site where you want web fonts to display. Example 6-1 shows how to do this.

Example 6-1. Example Google Web Fonts code

```
<html>
<head>

…

<script type="text/javascript">
```

```
      WebFontConfig = {
            google: { families: [ 'Roboto Slab:700', 'Roboto:400,400italic,700italic,
                      700' ] }
         };
      (function() {
                var wf = document.createElement('script');
                wf.src = ('https:' == document.location.protocol ? 'https' : 'http') +
                    '://ajax.googleapis.com/ajax/libs/webfont/1/webfont.js';
                wf.type = 'text/javascript';
                wf.async = 'true';
                var s = document.getElementsByTagName('script')[0];
                s.parentNode.insertBefore(wf, s);
         })();
   </script>

   <noscript>
      <link href='http://fonts.googleapis.com/css?family=Roboto+Slab:700|Roboto:400,
                400italic,700italic,700' rel='stylesheet' type='text/css'>
   </noscript>
```

This code and related bits and bobs can be found on the Google Fonts site (*http://bit.ly/ rt-foutfonts*). You'll find both the CSS and JavaScript methods there, along with information on download size and how to reference the fonts. While you're there, you may as well grab the sample font declarations to use in your CSS:

```
font-family: 'Roboto Slab', serif;
font-family: 'Roboto', sans-serif;
```

(We'll work out how to best use this in just a bit.)

Finally, you should make a quick detour (*http://bit.ly/rt-wfload*) to have a look at the README page showcasing the code required to use the Web Font Loader with various platforms. It's worth noting that while it may be good practice to put much of your JavaScript in the bottom of your page so you don't block loading, my preference is to keep all web font-related JavaScript ensconced in the <head> section (as long as you're loading asynchronously) so font loading gets started faster.

With that we've done several things: we've embedded the code to trigger the Web Font Loader, given it the fonts we want to load, set it to load asynchronously so it doesn't block the rest of the page loading, and included the aforementioned clever little bit of <noscript> code to load the fonts via CSS should JavaScript not be available. That's actually all that's necessary in the page itself. Not so bad, right? Our sample page in Figure 6-4 does have some extra bits in it (a JavaScript bit to add and remove classes and a couple of buttons to trigger them), but those are there to allow us to turn some features on and off, and to see just how it will look in action. The rest is all in our CSS file.

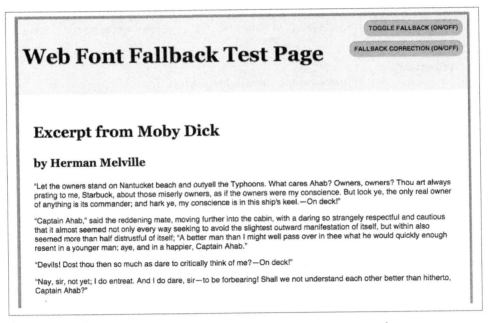

Figure 6-4. Sample page with web fonts not loaded, no correction in place

Since we're leveraging font events to add the wf-inactive and wf-active classes, we can dive into our CSS. We'll start with the basic styles for text on the page based on how we want the page to render with our selected web fonts:

```
body, th, td, input, textarea {
    font-family: 'Roboto', Helvetica, 'Lucida Sans', 'Lucida Grande',
    'Lucida Sans Unicode', sans-serif;
    font-size: 1em;
    letter-spacing: normal;
    line-height: 1.4em;
}
```

This will be the base, and it's applied either once the font event "loading" classes are removed, or when JavaScript is disabled and the fonts are loaded via CSS instead. However, we want to leverage the font events when possible, so we then list this alternate style that is called once the Web Font Loader has inserted the class indicating that web fonts are loading but not yet active (.wf-inactive):

```
.wf-inactive body, .wf-inactive th, .wf-inactive td, .wf-inactive input,
.wf-inactive textarea {
    font-family: Helvetica, "Lucida Sans","Lucida Grande",
                "Lucida Sans Unicode", sans-serif;
    font-size: 1em;
        letter-spacing: 0.0035em;
        line-height: 1.4em;
}
```

Notice a few key differences between the first set of declarations and the second: when .wf-inactive is added, we set the fonts without the web font listed and adjust the letter-spacing. We could also alter the font-size and increase the line-height at this point. These adjustments were easy to make with our demo page because we've added a toggle link in the top right corner to turn the web fonts on and off. If you give our demo page a look and try it out, you'll see that it's quite close—but likely not exact in our goal of "no reflow in any browser." You may be shocked to hear this, but apparently a pixel is not quite a pixel when it comes to implementing letter-spacing —*despite its having been around since CSS1*. I know, hard to believe.

So we have to fiddle with the fallback values of the second block and test it out in a number of browsers until we are close enough (see Figure 6-5). Mark it down along with horseshoes as one of the few places where "close enough" still scores you points. I've done the same in our demo with H1, H2, and H3 headers as examples, but you'll have to adapt this to your own workflow and CSS in order to ensure you've covered all your bases. Then test, test, test! You'll find that some browsers render letter-spacing smaller, some larger.

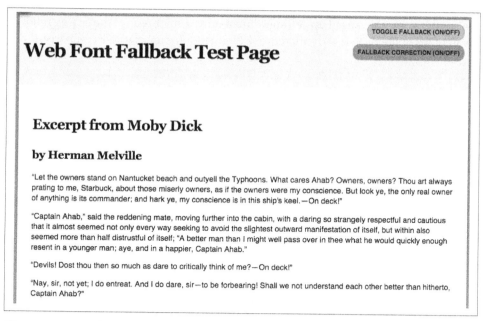

Figure 6-5. Sample page with web fonts not loaded but correction in place

Progressive Enhancement or Graceful Degradation?

One could argue that in order to properly address the page from a Progressive Enhancement point of view you should have your base CSS be the "fallback-tuned" version.

But with almost every web font service, you can address the potential lack of JavaScript with a CSS-only embedding link wrapped in a standard <noscript> block. With that in mind, I'd say this is indeed the proper base writeup. Because it relies upon JavaScript to enable the font event classes at all, the "fallback-corrected" CSS would actually be the "enhanced" bits and therefore should be added only when the font events are actually present.

The bigger issue actually may be that if you opt for the "fallback-tuned" no-web-font CSS as your base and only swap in the web-font-specific CSS when the wf-active class is present, users won't get web fonts at all even though their browser supports them. Just because there's no JavaScript that doesn't mean no web font support!

Lastly, it's worth calling out the most basic observation: why are we specifying CSS that uses a different font stack in the first place? The whole point of listing several fonts in order is so that the browser will load the next one if the first is not available! Well, this is where we must choose to balance true web standards and progressive enhancement with better user experience.

As we learned earlier, nearly all browser vendors have implemented an up to three-second delay when waiting for web fonts to load. Just leaving it at that means we can't do anything to either speed up getting content on screen or reduce the jarring reflow of content when the page is re-rendered. See Figure 6-6 for an example comparison.

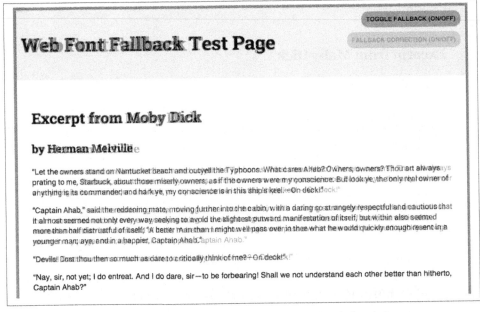

Figure 6-6. Overlay showing corrected fallbacks and final loaded web fonts

To put this in practice yourself, follow the previous samples, and while you're developing your HTML and CSS, include the handy toggle code from the demo so you can test your adjustments. Simply remove it when you're done. If you're developing in a CMS, you could even add the toggle as a block with all the necessary code, and simply turn it on whenever you need it. The demo is liberally sprinkled with helpful comments—just give it a try. It's not too hard, and the benefits will be noticed (or better yet, not noticed) with every page load.

CHAPTER 7

Proportion: Make It Scale, Make It Right

In case you haven't figured it out by now, I'll come clean here: I'm a big believer in Responsive Web Design. It's the only way I know to provide the best experience across the increasingly fragmented landscape of devices and capabilities that is the new normal on the Web today. But most of the advice you'll find about Responsive Design ignores relative scale in typography.

I find that really jarring, because in my experience, it's not just the absolute sizes of your type and spacing that must change as screen sizes shrink; the proportions between them must change, as well. So I've come up with a responsive relative scale to help you achieve a more readable page regardless of device or resolution.

Code Sample

Download the source code to follow along as we go.

View demo: *http://bit.ly/rt-demo-prop*

Download code: *http://bit.ly/rt-code-prop*

Out of Step and Size

For many of us, once we calculate a balanced and readable typographic scale and rhythm for our initial design, we turn our attention to tweaking floats and widths in the layout for other breakpoints.

What often gets missed is proportion. On every device, our h1s are three times (3em) the size of the body, every h2 is 2.25em, and so on.

The problem is that as the screen size shrinks and fewer elements are visible, the relative scale between elements becomes exaggerated. What's needed is greater subtlety and flexibility to maintain a more balanced proportion and better readability across all experiences.

A More Modern Measured Scale

Starting with the well-tested set of norms set out by Robert Bringhurst in his seminal work *The Elements of Typographic Style* (Hartley & Marks, 2002), I've spent some time refining those proportions across a number of different devices. In doing so, a sliding scale emerged that preserves the spirit of his recommendations but yields more balanced results across screen sizes.

I've based my scale on a relative type size of 1em for the <body> element, which (as I described in Chapter 6) will result in a size equivalent to 16px in virtually all browsers. In most typefaces this yields an accepted standard(ish) size for body copy. By working in relative units and using the <body> as my baseline, our trusty <p> will inherit that standard base for most of the content, and everything else will render in proportion to that no matter where it's displayed.

This is particularly important on smaller-screen devices, where the actual physical resolution is quite different from the reported size. By sticking with a 1em measurement, you're more likely to have appropriately scaled text based on the norms for each device and OS.

The main point is that while each of the breakpoints retains a consistent scale in its individual typographic hierarchy, as you move through the breakpoints, the scales vary as necessary (see Figure 7-1). For example: while body copy stays consistent at 100% or 1em, h1s might be set at 2em on small screens, 2.5em on tablet-size devices, and 3em on typical desktop screens.

	Print	Desktop (large)	Desktop	Tablet (large)	Tablet (small)	Phone
Body						
- Font size:	- 12pt	- 16px (1em)	- 16px (1em)	- 16px (1em)	- 16px (1em)	- 16px (1em)
- Line height:	- 1.25	- 1.375	- 1.375	- 1.375	- 1.25	- 1.375
- Line length:	- 60-75	- 60-75	- 60-75	- 60-75	- 60-75	- 60-75
H1						
- Font size:	- 36pt (3em)	- 48px (3em)	- 48px (3em)	- 40px (2.5em)	- 32px (2em)	- 32px (2em)
- Line height:	- 1.25	- 1.05	- 1.05	- 1.125	- 1.25	- 1.25
H2						
- Font size:	- 24pt (2em)	- 36px (2.25em)	- 36px (2.25em)	- 32px (2em)	- 26px (1.625em)	- 26px (1.625em)
- Line height:	- 1.25	- 1.25	- 1.25	- 1.25	- 1.15384615	- 1.15384615
H3						
- Font size:	- 18pt (1.5em)	- 28px (1.75em)	- 28px (1.75em)	- 24px (1.5em)	- 22px (1.375em)	- 22px (1.375em)
- Line height:	- 1.25	- 1.25	- 1.25	- 1.25	- 1.13636364	- 1.13636364
H4						
- Font size:	- 14pt (1.667em)	- 18px (1.125em)	- 18px (1.125em)	- 18px (1.125em)	- 18px (1.125em)	- 18px (1.125em)
- Line height:	- 1.25	- 1.25	- 1.25	- 1.222222	- 1.1111111	- 1.1111111
Blockquote						
- Font size:	- 24pt (2em)	- 24px (1.5em)	- 24px (1.5em)	- 24px (1.5em)	- 20px (1.25em)	- 20px (1.25em)
- Line height:	- 1.458333	- 1.4583333	- 1.4583333	- 1.4583333	- 1.25	- 1.25

Figure 7-1. Scaled values for headings and copy across print, desktop, and mobile devices

One Size Won't Rule Them All

Hearkening back to Bringhurst's tome, we're confronted with the "66 characters" rule: his recommended line length for maximum clarity, readability, and proportion in print (also endorsed by Richard Rutter in his adaptation of Bringhurst's work for the Web). To sum up the adaptation, for the web it's 16px (1em) for body copy size and a measure of 60 to 75 characters for line length of body text, while headers should be 48px (3em).

These recommendations are based on a number of factors, such as: how people tend to read by taking in groups of shapes at a time rather than individual letters and words; the ease or difficulty in following a line to the end and bringing your eye back to the start of the next line; and quickly understanding the relative importance of various levels of headings between blocks of copy. It works. It feels harmonious. It has the significant advantage of being familiar due to its common adoption. It is also, we must remember, based on a single-column print or desktop layout.

Unfortunately, the 66-character guideline breaks down when screen sizes radically change. The multicolumn design situations that Bringhurst discusses (such as with newspapers) are a closer match to the space constraints we face with smaller viewports, and for newspaper columns he recommends 40- to 50-character line lengths. However, we can't take this as an absolute rule either; 40 to 50 characters with comfortable margins on a 320-pixel-wide display ends up feeling a bit hard to read.

There must be a trade-off in how large the type appears and how many characters fit on a line. After a lot of experimentation, 35 to 40 characters per line on a typical smartphone seems to me to provide the best balance for more legible and readable text.

Of course once you begin altering line length, many other properties are affected.

We've talked a bit about line length, but let's have a look at line height as well for good measure. (Sorry, can't help having a few typographic puns slip through.) Line length must be balanced with line height (the vertical distance from one baseline of text to the next above or below) to give the eye an easy path back to start the next line. To ensure the best reading experience, you would generally want between 1.25 and 1.5 for a line height setting. That optimum setting varies as line length changes.

Generally you can have a slightly more open line height on larger screens, but often you may want to tighten things up on the smallest devices. Shorter line lengths make it easier for the eye to travel back to the start of the next line without quite as much height, with the added bonus of being able to present a bit more content on screen.

Hyphenation

It's worth noting that when working with shorter line lengths, you are more likely to run into hyphenation as an issue. You can control it relatively well, though, with CSS. It's good practice to specifically enable it on the smallest screens, and you may want to actually disable it on larger ones (unless you're justifying your type, but that's another issue. I won't judge).

While there are still some browser prefixes required for older versions, the CSS is relatively simple:

```
p {
    hyphens: auto;
}
@media only screen and (min-width: 45em) {
    p {
        hyphens: none;
    }
}
```

Take It from the Top

Don't forget that headings also need quite a bit of attention, because a single scale simply doesn't work for all viewports.

For example, a heading set to 3em looks normal and proportionate relative to body copy on a desktop, but it tends to look oversized and clownish when viewed on a very small screen because it's not competing with as much white space and other page elements (see Figure 7-2).

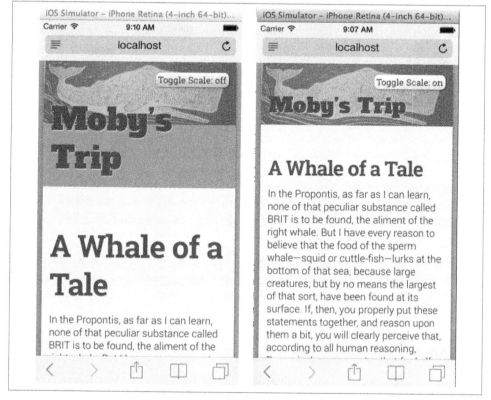

Figure 7-2. A comparison of mobile headers with and without correction

On my scale, the ratio between the body text and headers changes as we move from desktop to tablet to smartphone. The H1s, for example, reduce from 3em to 2.5em to 2em as the viewports shrink. I've built a sample page to show you how this looks in situ (see Figure 7-3). If you resize its window, you'll see the scale of the headers change as the viewport changes. (Or you can toggle the page to off, to quickly see how awful a single scale looks at various breakpoints). These heading values may not be science, but they seem to feel right and pass the "squint test" nicely. (OK, so the squint test isn't scientific either, but squinting at your design works well for seeing which elements still stand out.)

Figure 7-3. Comparison of desktop, tablet, and phone views

More subtle proportions at smaller breakpoints mean there may be less size distinction among all the heading levels, but font size is only one element of the design. You can still establish good visual hierarchy and the desired contrast using color and font variants.

Also remember that while headings rarely wrap on desktops, they likely will on smaller devices, so you must carefully choose the appropriate `line-height` for headings. Otherwise, that spacing between headings and the elements that follow will look just as goofy on mobile as an oversized font!

Respect the White Space

Shorter line lengths can permit tighter line height, but this must be balanced by dedicating more of the viewport to text. However, when adapting a design for smaller viewports, often the tendency is to preserve elements of the background and original design. This results in considerable space on either side of the content being devoted to design elements like background photos or textures, content panels offset from backgrounds with shadows, etc. The result is not enough space for type, which ends up either too small or too ragged, with choppy line lengths and a rough reading experience.

By reducing margins outside the main content area (like when there's a background color or texture and a main content area, each with its own margins), you can give more space for content, allowing for slightly longer lines of text. On a small screen I tend to get rid of any color or texture in the body and let the content area go all the way to the edge—a simple single margin. At 320 pixels wide, we need all of the horizontal space we can get to achieve readable copy!

Implementing the Scale

You can apply these differing ratios easily using media queries in your CSS, right along with the rest of your responsive design bits. Depending on your design and how many breakpoints you're targeting, you may want to tweak intermediate ratios for tablets. I tend to group these CSS rules in a single file and load it (or compile it) in between redefining basic HTML elements and any final CSS modules defined for specific usage on the site.

Note that in my sample page's CSS I've also tried to preserve a reasonable vertical rhythm by making margins above and below relate to line height for body copy, and set the line heights for headings to a number with a relationship to that, as well. Comments are inline to explain the math.

And so…

Bear in mind: every typeface is different, as is every design—so this scale won't work *exactly* the same way for every project. But it does give you a good starting point to help maintain the intent and hierarchy of your design as it travels from one screen to the next.

CHAPTER 8

Polish: Finessing the Fine Points

Now that we've covered the basics of type choice and implementation, it's good to remind ourselves that this is the beginning of our typographic work, not the end! Well, it could be, and you'd still be far ahead of most sites on the Web these days. But there's a lot more you can do to enrich the reading experience.

Code Sample

Download the source code to follow along and try this yourself.

View demo: *http://bit.ly/rt-demo-polish*

Download code: *http://bit.ly/rt-code-polish*

Start with the Details—Then Get Really Specific

Beyond choosing good typefaces, a number of other elements in your typographic design influence aesthetics and readability. Some of these are tied to your design, such as line length; others are more tied to the nature of fluid design or more traditional elements of good typography. Orphans are a good example of the latter complicated by the former: leaving a single word on a line at the end of a paragraph. This is an aesthetic faux pas easily prevented in print but deceptively difficult when the length of your lines of text keep changing on every device.

While it's not foolproof, there is something you can do to prevent orphans relatively easily. It may be true that the Web and responsible standards-based approaches to designing require flexibility on the part of the site owner and designer, but there is no need to throw up your hands and give up on using type well altogether.

Little Orphan

Just because line lengths and sizes change doesn't mean you can't help the orphans. Take a little time from your day and experiment with adding a *nonbreaking space* (or) between the last two words of any <p> to magically fix that typographic heartbreak (see Figure 8-1). Typogrify (*http://bit.ly/rt-tpgrfy*), created by Christian Metts, is a great little library that not only will do this for you on-the-fly but also includes automatic substitution of real quotation marks (single and double), encoding of special characters and even replacement of things like a -- (double hyphen) with a true "en" dash.

I first came across the above quote during my ado
to Carl Jung, and almost thirty years later it remair
sentiment. Does it speak to my fatalist tendencies
rather believe that it provides me the leeway to try
incapacitating fear of failure. Anxieties abound wt
forward - especially when accompanied by an unc
there's sturdy enough ground beneath us. But if w
probability of lessons learned, regardless of our st
challenges, then doesn't that soften the blow of pe
hard?

These are the thoughts running through my head a
journey.

I first came across the above quote during my adolescent introduction to Carl Jung, and almost thirty years later it remains a cherished sentiment. Does it speak to my fatalist tendencies? Maybe. But I'd rather believe that it provides me the leeway to try new paths without an incapacitating fear of failure. Anxieties abound when taking a new step forward - especially when accompanied by an uncertainty as to whether there's sturdy enough ground beneath us. But if we focus on the probability of lessons learned, regardless of our successes or challenges, then doesn't that soften the blow of possibly falling too hard?

These are the thoughts running through my head as I embark upon a new journey.

Figure 8-1. Caution: editors may spontaneously kiss you when you show them how you can automatically prevent orphans in their CMS

If you're using Drupal, there's even a module for that (*http://bit.ly/rt-tpgrfy-drupal*). There's a plugin for WordPress (*http://bit.ly/rt-tpgrfy-wp*), but as of this writing it has not been updated in quite some time. Aaron Gustafson has also created a port for Expression Engine (*http://bit.ly/rt-tpgrfy-ee*).

Recently, though, I came across a nifty bit of coding from Nathan Ford that performs a similar function on the client side using JavaScript (*http://bit.ly/rt-widotamer*). Because it's handled in JavaScript, it makes quite an easy addition to almost any website or CMS without requiring any editing or alteration of the content itself. It even allows you to specify how many characters you want as the minimum length on the last line of a paragraph, so you can opt for something longer than just two words.

When Is an ff Not an ff?

As I've said earlier in the book, words may have meaning, but letters have emotion. Great typography has long had an arsenal of special tools to handle special circumstances and requirements which greatly enhance the visual quality and readability of really well-set type. OpenType features are one of those tools, and they add greater depth and variety by expanding the character sets of OT-enabled typefaces.

These include such typographic delights as ligatures, swashes, stylistic alternates, and even real kerning (see Figure 8-2). You can expand your emotional vocabulary by exploring all of these marvelous features; there's no reason to stop with just the typeface.

Figure 8-2. Examples of standard and discretionary ligatures

Just what are all these typographic beauties? Well, for starters there are ligatures (including standard, discretionary, and contextual varieties). These are combinations of characters that historically tend to blend together when drawn or cut, such as ff, ffl, fi, or fj. Technically this is when the *hood* of the f is combined with the *tittle* of the lowercase "i" or "j," but you can see how it might become hard to keep a straight face when discussing the topic.

One of my personal favorites is the less common ligature for "ct" and "st," as seen in Adobe Caslon Pro, among others (shown in Figure 8-2). Then there are swashes, like those shown in Figure 8-3: lovely swoops and embellishments that add a truly distinctive character when put to good use.

> "The ungracious and ungrateful dog!" cried Starbuck; "he mocks and dares me with the very poor-box I filled for him, not five minutes ago!"—then in his old intense whisper—"Give way, greyhounds! Dog to it!"

Figure 8-3. Swashes and contextual swashes enabled in Fairbank, courtesy of Fonts.com

Other common features include stylistic alternates and various options for numerals, including tabular figures (evenly spaced and perfect for financial tables), fractions, and old-style figures (with both ascenders and descenders, to fit well with upper- and lowercase letters), as you can see in Figure 8-4.

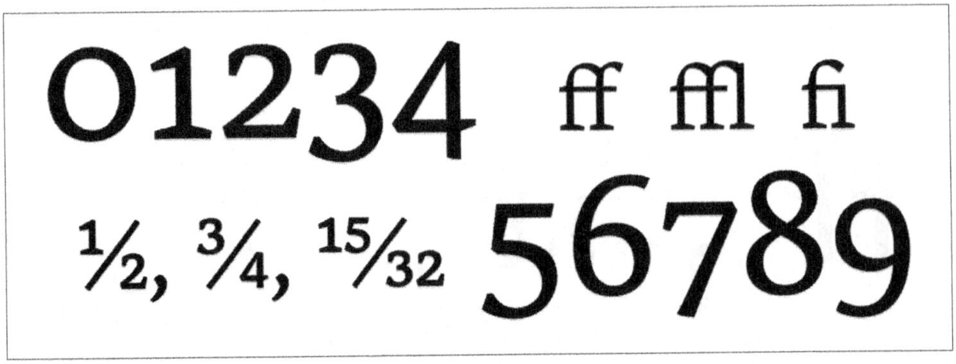

Figure 8-4. Ligatures, old-style numerals, and fractions

Then there are kerning tables. These are the values the type designer has set for spacing between each combination of letters in a given typeface, and incorporating those accurately makes an enormous difference. Kerning alone may be worth the price of admission, as I've always felt that browsers tend to do a fairly middling job of spacing type on screen (shown in Figure 8-5).

Figure 8-5. From top to bottom: no kerning, OpenType kerning enabled, and an overlay of both

A Hint of History

These characters and features have existed for centuries, but only recently have they become usable on the web. Ligatures were first seen in Sumerian manuscripts and many subsequent forms of writing and calligraphy. With the advent of movable type, ligatures were used to improve letterspacing to allow spacing tighter than otherwise separate blocks of type would allow.

Many of these features fell out of favor with the advent of photo- and then computer-based typesetting. It's only been in recent years that better font formats have made them available again, and they've been finding their way back into favor.

With the advent of OpenType (or more correctly Open Font Format) on the desktop and its derivative Web Open Font Format (for, you guessed it, use on the Web) there finally exists a pair of font formats that can be used nearly universally. The significance here is these formats support a much wider array of characters and features, for finer typographic control than ever before.

As in all things Web, use of these features is supported at varying levels in all the major browsers, but it's prevalent enough now to be worth serious consideration and use.

The CSS required has been around for a few years and is part of the CSS3 type module. Unfortunately, it's been slow progress to get wide enough support for the WOFF format, so it follows that browser implementation and support has evolved slowly, as well. It's worth noting that the current versions of every major shipping browser that supports `@font-face` also supports OpenType features. You can check on how far back that support extends very easily on Can I Use (*http://caniuse.com/#search=woff*).

Thankfully, even though support and syntax vary, tools like Sass can help make it more practical to give it a try, and if the syntax doesn't work or the feature is unsupported, the user just ends up with normal text. Of course, there's always a catch: enabling Open-Type features does increase the file size, but with care and caching it doesn't have to be a performance killer.

What With Issues of Syntax and File Size, Why Bother?

Design is about communication, but people make judgments about usability based on aesthetics (I'll point you again to Jennifer Chen's excellent article on Usability.gov (*http://bit.ly/rt-aesthetics*) titled "The Impact of Aesthetics on Attitudes Towards Websites"). So it behooves us to pull out all the stops in how we communicate with our typographic choices. Furthermore, you must remember we read by scanning groups of shapes, not individual letters. So the smoother the flow and easier it is to grasp groups of letters and understand them as words and phrases, the faster the user will comprehend the message you are trying to get across. And you'll be doing it with style.

The Details, Please

Once you have included a font in your site that has OpenType features enabled, using them in your CSS is fairly straightforward. The official CSS3 syntax looks like this:

```
p {
    font-feature-settings: "liga" 1, "frac" 1;
}
```

This code turns on both standard ligatures and fractions, if those features are available. Due to syntax variations, the safer way to include them actually looks more like this:

```
p {
    -moz-font-feature-settings :   "liga=1", "frac=1";
    -moz-font-feature-settings :   "liga" 1, "frac" 1;
    -webkit-font-feature-settings : "liga" 1, "frac" 1;
    -ms-font-feature-settings : "liga=1", "frac=1";
    -o-font-feature-settings : "liga" 1, "frac" 1;
    font-feature-settings : "liga" 1, "frac" 1;
}
```

Yes, I realize Firefox is in here twice. Ah, Web. That's due to a syntax change somewhere around Firefox 14.

Here's a more complete list of what features exist and how to reference them:

Reference:

```
"c2sc" : small caps from caps
"calt" : contextual alternates
"clig" : contextual ligatures
"dlig" : discretionary ligatures
"hist" : historical character alternatives
"hlig" : historical ligatures
"kern" : enable use of embedded kerning table
"liga" : common ligatures
"nalt" : alternate annotation
"salt" : stylistic alternatives
"smcp" : small caps
"ss01" : alternate stylistic set 1
"ss02" : alternate stylistic set 2
"ss03" : alternate stylistic set 3
"ss04" : alternate stylistic set 4
"ss05" : alternate stylistic set 5
"swsh" : swashes
"zero" : slashed-zero
```

The following options require a sort of conditional logic (at least in your own mind), as you can really only enable one of these pairs at a time:

Number case:

```
"lnum" : lining numbers
```

or

```
"onum" : oldstyle numbers
```

Number spacing:

```
    "pnum" : proportional
```

or

```
    "tnum" : tabular (for lining up rows of numbers like financials)
```

Fractions:

```
    "frac" : normal fractions
```

or

```
    "afrc" : alternate fractions
```

Don't want to remember all that? If you use Sass, I've got a mixin for you (*http://bit.ly/jpsassotf*) (this provides the previous list and does all the code writing for you). Rich Rutter also provides a fantastic tool (*http://bit.ly/rt-clagnutcss3*) that allows you to experiment with Fontdeck web fonts and toggle lots of different OpenType features (*http://bit.ly/rt-clagnutcss3*).

For a more exhaustive list, Adobe has one here: *http://bit.ly/rt-adobeotf.*

A Reasoned Approach

Every element of your design must be there for a reason, but it's important to remember that sometimes that reason is simply for greater beauty. And that's OK. The nice thing about OpenType features is they fall back to regular type all on their own, so they're pretty safe to add to your design, and the level of polish they add can be quite noticeable. With greater emphasis on readability and increased pixel density and screen quality, more and more users are reading longer content online.

That means the benefits in readability from better typography can quickly translate into increased loyalty, greater perceived usability, and even parades of unicorns and puppies. (OK, maybe that last one is an exaggeration, but you do get some bonus points for using code so effectively to improve your design!)

One More for the Road (or the Beginning of Your Paragraph)

One of the most classic typographic design techniques is the large initial capital letter at the beginning of a page or chapter (see Figure 8-6). It's a very noticeable design element, but one not often seen on the Web. It's a shame, as it's actually not that hard to do, doesn't require too much in terms of browser support, and can be accomplished without adding any more markup to your content. By taking advantage of two simple techniques, you can cover just about all browser combinations. The first and more modern approach is to use something like this, which will style just the first letter of the first p in the `.content` area of the page:

```
.content p:first-of-type:first-letter {
    font-size: 3em;
        font-family: "Playfair Display", Georgia, "Times New Roman";
        line-height: 0.9em;
        float: left;
        padding-right: 0.15em;


}
```

A Whale of an Affliction

I n the Propontis, as far as I can learn, none of that peculiar substance called BRIT is to be found, the aliment of the right whale. But I have every reason to believe that the food of the sperm whale—**squid or cuttle-fish**—lurks at the bottom of that sea, because large creatures, but by no means the largest of that sort, have been found at its surface. If, then, you properly put these statements together, and reason upon them a bit, you will clearly perceive that, according to all human reasoning, Procopius's sea-monster, that for half a century stove the ships of a Roman Emperor, must in all probability have been a sperm whale.

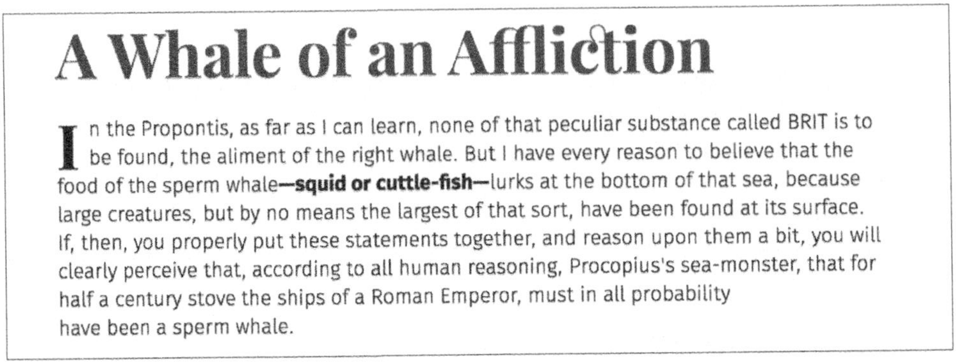

Figure 8-6. A large initial cap

The only drawback is that the pseudoselector :first-of-type is only supported in IE versions 9 and later. An alternative would be to tie into conditional classes in your html element. The sample code uses a set of conditionally loaded versions of the html element that are only utilized by IE 9 and below. With these you can be sure that if someone is using one of those older versions of IE, they will have a .lt-ie9 class present, allowing you to use an alternative bit of HTML. Something like this should work a treat:

```
.lt-ie9 .content h1 + p:first-letter {
    font-size: 3em;
    font-family: "Playfair Display", Georgia, "Times New Roman";
        line-height: 0.9em;
        float: left;
        padding-right: 0.15em;
}
```

While not the prettiest solution, this does work to set the first letter of the first p following the h1 in the .content area. It's a bit overly tied to the HTML structure of the page for our liking, but as long as the markup structure is consistent, it should work just fine. By scoping it with the .lt-ie9 class, at least we restrict our shame to a much more limited set of users.

Pulling It All Together

Each of the techniques in this chapter can make a noticeable difference on your site. By layering them together, you can create rich, textured reading experiences that can rival the finest books. Well, we still can't recreate the musty-paper-and-ink smell—but I'm sure there's a Kickstarter for that.

CHAPTER 9

Notes, Notions, and Sending You on Your Way

This chapter is a bit of a catchall, but I had to include some useful tips and tidbits that don't fit neatly into the other chapters.

Dynamic Scaling: Great for Layout, Not So Great for Type

Although there are JavaScript libraries and measurement units that allow you to fit text to a specific area, varying size and scale accordingly, I think using them is generally not a good idea, even for headline and display text. Doing so changes the relative proportion between headings and body copy, which can have a detrimental effect on your design.

As I mentioned several times already I'm sure, I firmly believe that in most cases you should leave the size of your body copy alone, allowing the device manufacturer and OS vendor to determine what's best in that environment. It follows that headings should maintain a predictable scale relationship with the body copy, imparting appropriate hierarchy and importance based on that relationship. Changing heading size dynamically (using FitText.js or `viewport-width`) changes that hierarchy, therefore changing the imparted meaning. And that undermines your design.

Windows XP: Killing Good Typography Since 2001

I talked a bit about the, ahem, challenges we face with type rendering in older versions of Windows and IE, but I think it's been too easily brushed aside lately in common discussion. The ugly truth is that Windows XP still represents roughly 40% of Microsoft's installed base worldwide, and globally IE 8 still accounts for over 20% of the traffic on the Web.

So deal with it we must. Quite often you'll find everything working quite nicely everywhere else, but your type will look awful, spindly, and jagged in IE 8 and earlier versions. What's a poor designer to do? Well, here are a few tips to get you started.

Don't Turn Around—uh-oh (Just Turn a Little Bit)

Rotating a text element 1/10,000 of a percent (really) can force Windows to treat the text like a graphic and apply smoothing that otherwise would go missing. Strange, esoteric—and yet effective. You can read more about it here: *http://bit.ly/rt-ierotate* (but be sure to test thoroughly, as sometimes it can end up just making things muddy).

A Shadow Without Sunshine

Another trick is to apply a text shadow with 0% opacity. It doesn't work so well if the type is on a background that has any kind of transparency, but if it's on a solid color it can work quite well.

Clearly Off-Kilter

This one can work is for those special situations where the font-smoothing technology ClearType actually makes things worse. It's a nifty little trick (*http://bit.ly/rt-ietricks*):

```
h1 {
    font-family: 'Roboto', Arial, Sans-Serif;
        filter: progid:DXImageTransform.Microsoft.
AlphaImageLoader(src=hIEfix.png,sizingMethod=crop);
    zoom: 1;
}
```

Again, this should be tested with your particular typefaces, but sometimes you have to try a few different approaches to find just the right balance of speed, quality, and compatibility.

These tricks tend to be appropriate only for headers or other short bits of text—there often isn't much you can do if the text you've selected for the body doesn't render well. The good news is that at smaller sizes, the problems are generally less apparent. But again: there's no substitute for testing!

Icon Fonts

Icon fonts have become tremendously popular in the past few years, and in general I've been a really big fan. This is the practice of taking icons that are used in your design for things like social media platforms, UI controls, search buttons, and the like and converting them from vector artwork form into an actual font (see Figure 9-1). Then you can use @font-face to embed them and use them in your site, allowing for coloring, scaling, and any other effects you can apply to text of any sort with CSS. Lightweight, scalable, and portable. What's not to like?

Figure 9-1. Examples of icons from FontAwesome.io

But there's a real potential issue with relying upon them: what about when web fonts don't load? If the icons are providing critical functions in your design, such as a magnifying glass being used as a search form button, it's a major issue if they don't load. There are some ways you can provide fallbacks, but they're not all ideal and none of them are perfect.

If the goal is lightweight, scalable, and portable icons, there is an alternative: SVG. Or better yet, SVG with PNG fallback for platforms that don't support SVG (IE 8 and earlier and Android 2.3 and earlier, primarily). Thankfully, the good folks at Filament Group have stepped in with Grumpicon (*http://bit.ly/rt-grump*), a brilliant web app that takes a folder of SVG icons (which you can save straight out of Illustrator) and converts them to a tidy download of icon files, fallbacks, and all the code you need to use them in your site. All for the price of, well, nothing. It's free.

If you have no visitors from Africa, India, Asia, or anywhere else that Opera Mini may be the norm, you may feel fine about using an icon font. And to be honest, I've continued to use them myself, though on my current projects I may try out this new approach. I may be an old dog, but I do like to learn new tricks. Which is good, because in this industry it really pays to be committed to learning new things.

Wrap It Up and Put a Bow on It

So there you have it. Responsive Typography explained, illustrated, and annotated. While it's impossible to show you everything (I've had to revise many sections just during the time I've been writing this, as specs and support have changed so frequently), I hope this serves as a good primer. Performance, progression, proportion, and polish are the main tenets.

Paying mind to those will take you a long way, and hopefully your own curiosity will take you even further. Thankfully, there are other resources as well, either in print or coming soon. One book will never supply all the answers, but I certainly hope this one has given you more than a few.

The examples presented are all real: even the ones shown as an image are generated from live HTML and CSS. And even if you don't incorporate every trick and tidbit from the book in every project, just using a few will dramatically improve the overall experience. Each time it gets easier and quicker, especially if you tend to work with a particular CMS or starting point. Building in the basics of good typography from the start is always quicker, and doing so also leaves more time for deeper thinking and finer finesse.

Remember: type is your voice. Speak eloquently.

Web Font Services

This list describes a number of vendors and services, with some notes on their use. All have some sort of free account to start with, so the barrier to entry is pretty low to get started and try it out. It's worth noting that most services can be used on multiple domains with a single monthly subscription, so agencies can maintain multiple accounts in order to find the best combinations of available fonts and pricing levels for just about any size project.

Fontdeck.com

Fontdeck (*http://fontdeck.com*) was one of the first services to launch, having been conceived by Jon Tan and Richard Rutter in 2009. It has a really elegant interface, a comprehensive tagging system for search, flexible pricing, and the best implementation of OpenType feature support I've found thus far. Fontdeck uses its tags to surface typefaces that have OpenType features enabled (*http://bit.ly/rt-fdot*) and shows you which Open-Type features are supported on each typeface detail page. Very handy. Fontdeck cofounder Rich Rutter's commitment to better typography on the Web is inspiring, and it's clear that there will be more features to come from the service.

Fonts.com

Also one of the early launches, Fonts.com (*http://fonts.com*) from Monotype was one of the most prolific of the services with regard to the number of fonts available: launching with about 7,500 and quickly growing to more than 30,000. It is still one of the only services to provide both JavaScript and CSS methods of embedding, and it has always been incredibly supportive of my own efforts and those of the web community as a whole. Fonts.com lets you search typefaces by a number of criteria, including availability of OpenType features (*http://bit.ly/rt-fcot*). It also offers an innovative way to include features in the web interface on assigned selectors, making it unnecessary to include your own CSS. Johnathan Zsittnik, eCommerce Marketing Manager at Monotype, let me know that they've been hard at work enabling more OpenType features in more fonts all the time, with more discoverability of those enabled fonts in the works, as well.

Google.com/fonts

The Google Web Font service is free to use, and has a fairly extensive library of open source fonts. You do have to test thoroughly to be sure that the fonts are hinted well and render nicely on all platforms, and there may not be as many weights and variants available, but there are some real gems worth exploring. I've used them extensively in these demos in order to make the code as portable as possible: Roboto, Roboto Slab, Merriweather, Open Sans, and Source Sans are all excellent typefaces that stand up well everywhere I've tested them.

Adobe Typekit.com

Adobe Typekit (*http://typekit.com*) was the first service to launch and was a complete game-changer for many designers, who then flocked to the service in droves. It has always had very user-friendly search, as well as one of the best blogs for both inspiration and education. Like the other sites mentioned here, Typekit supports OpenType features on select typefaces. While at this time there isn't an easy way to know what fonts support them or which features are supported on a given typeface, that seems destined to change. Elliot Jay Stocks, creative director at Typekit, let me know that the team has plans for the very near future to highlight and utilize OpenType features to a much greater extent.

Typography.com

Hoefler & Co. launched its Cloud Typography (*http://typography.com*) service publicly in 2013 after a lengthy (and much coveted) beta period, and it was worth the wait. It's one of the most "tunable" services with regard to including only what you want, and the quality is really outstanding. It's one of the only services to work with just its own creations, but given the demand for its typefaces and how reasonable the pricing is, that seems to be just fine. Not surprisingly, it also supports OpenType features in its typefaces, with some of the most extensive and fine-grained controls over exactly which features you want to enable. This gives you a bit more control over the size of the eventual download. Some good documentation is available from their user guide (*http://bit.ly/rt-hcsubset*).

WebINK.com

Coming from a legendary background in font management, it's not that big a surprise that Extensis launched its own service very early on. It stands apart in its pricing: all other services price based upon page views; WebINK (*http://webink.com*) prices based on unique visitors. This is a tremendous benefit for sites that have strong engagement with a loyal user base. It supports OpenType features as well, and has a support page listing all of the fonts that support them.

Jim Kidwell, Extensis's product marketing manager, did weigh in that more is on the drawing board, so we'll have to wait and see what's next. For now though you can also take in Thomas Phinney's excellent post (*http://bit.ly/rt-exotf*) on using OpenType features. (Unfortunately, as of June 2014 Extensis announced they were shutting down the WebINK service.)

Webtype.com

Launched in late 2010, Webtype (*http://webtype.com*) is a partnership between Font Bureau, Roger Black, and Peter van Blokland. Pricing is similar to most (based on page views per month). I haven't used this one personally, but I know many top designers who have and love it.

Responsive Typography and Web Fonts in Email

I have to admit that with all of the other difficulties we face designing and developing HTML emails, it may seem a bit daft to throw web fonts into the mix. But I've heard recently from some newsletter publishers that over 80% of their recipients can view web fonts in their email clients, so I decided it made sense to at least bring it up.

There are two main issues why web fonts don't work in email (besides the obvious: that email clients can't even spell web standards): many email clients, especially the web-based ones, strip out JavaScript and limit other external resources; and many web font services tie the use of their fonts to a URL, and there is no URL that corresponds to your inbox! That means that in many cases the web fonts would never be served, even if the HTML, CSS, and JavaScript survived intact.

You can use Google Web Fonts, as they don't have that kind of restriction, or you can try using self-hosted fonts. That may be more likely to work.

The following article from Campaign Monitor has some very good pointers and data, though it will always be evolving. The one from MailChimp at this time is not quite as comprehensive, but you can be sure that both vendors will be keeping tabs on the state of support and writing about it often.

Beyond web fonts, there are still many things you can do to make your emails responsive. While it's outside the purview of this book to dive too deeply into that code, if you are responsible for designing and/or producing responsive email, this is a great place to start.

Resources

- "Responsive Email Design" from Campaign Monitor (*http://bit.ly/rt-rdemailcm*)

- "Web Fonts in Email" from Campaign Monitor (*http://bit.ly/rt-emailcm*)
- "Responsive Email" from MailChimp (*http://bit.ly/rt-rdemailmc*)
- "Typography in Email" from MailChimp (*http://bit.ly/rt-emailmc*)

Index

We'd like to hear your suggestions for improving our indexes. Send email to index@oreilly.com.

About the Author

Jason Pamental has been blending design and technology since the early days of Mosaic and Netscape. Through years in both creative and technical leadership roles for Fortune 100 clients, well-renowned professional sporting sites, and a host of other clients large and small, Jason brings in-depth experience in a broad range of disciplines. Ranging from branding, print design, all aspects of web design and development, and even data-center infrastructure management, he most enjoys challenges that draw upon all of his diverse experiences to truly transform his clients' businesses. In recent years, besides co-founding H+W Design (*http://www.hwdesignco.com*), he's begun sharing more of his unsolicited advice with the Drupal community, speaking and teaching workshops at various web conferences, and writing on sites like Fonts.com (*http://www.fonts.com*) and Typecast.com (*http://www.typecast.com*) about things he's done wrong, in the hopes that others might fare just a bit better than he did.

Colophon

The animal on the cover of *Responsive Typography* is a crested pelican (*Pelecanus erythrorhynchos*). This pelican is a large aquatic bird found in interior North America during breeding season, and on the coasts, in the south, and Central and South America during the winter.

This bird is very large and plump, averaging a length of 50–70 inches, much of which is its beak, which measures about 11.3–15.2 inches in males and 10.3–14.2 inches in females. Its wingspan ranges from 95–120 inches, which allows the bird to use soaring flight for migration. They can weigh between 9.2–30 lb, but average around 11–20 lb. Males and females are identical except for size.

From early spring to mid-late summer, when breeding season ends, their breast feathers take on a yellowish hue. Afterward, it moults into its eclipse plumage—the upper head has a grey hue and blackish feathers grow between the wispy white crest. The pelican's bill is large and flat on top with a large throat sac on the bottom. During breeding season, their bills are bright orange, matching the iris (the skin around the eye) and its feet; during this time, there is a flattened horn on the upper bill.

The pelican nests in colonies of several hundred pairs. About 10–20% of the population uses Gunnison Island in the Great Salt Lake as a nesting ground. This pelican catches its prey while swimming; each bird can eat up to four pounds of food each day, consisting mostly of fish like carp, shiners, perch, and rainbow trout. They also eat some crayfish and amphibians and occasionally larval salamanders. The pelicans like to feed in groups, cooperating and corralling fish to one another. In deeper waters, where fish can escape by diving out of reach, they prefer to feed alone.

Pelicans are colonial breeds, with up to 5,000 pairs per site. Breeding season begins in March or April and nesting begins in early April to early June. Their nests are a shallow depression of scraped ground, with twigs and sticks gathered inside. After about a week of courting and building the nest, the female lays a clutch of eggs—usually two to three, sometimes one, sometimes up to six. Incubation includes both parents and lasts about a month. About three to four weeks after hatching, the young leave the nest; usually only one young survives per next. The young spend their time learning to fly and moulting into immature plumage. The parents care for their offspring for three more weeks, then the family separates.

This species is protected by the Migratory Bird Treaty Act of 1918, and is covered by the California Department of Fish and Game protective status and is a California species of special concern. Globally, this species is listed as one of least concern by the IUCN. Habitat loss is destructive to nesting, with flooding and drought as recurring challenges. Human-related stress to the species includes entanglement in fishing gear and poaching. The excessive spraying of DDT and other organochlorides in agriculture as well as erosion at breeding colonies have both provided to the decline in pelican population in the mid-20th century.

Many of the animals on O'Reilly covers are endangered; all of them are important to the world. To learn more about how you can help, go to animals.oreilly.com.

The cover image is from *Beauties of Land and Sea*. The cover fonts are URW Typewriter and Guardian Sans. The text font is Adobe Minion Pro; the heading font is Adobe Myriad Condensed; and the code font is Dalton Maag's Ubuntu Mono.

Have it your way.

CPSIA information can be obtained at www.ICGtesting.com
Printed in the USA
BVOW08s1325071214

378323BV00006B/17/P